For Marcella

Queer and Indecent

Queer and Indecent

An Introduction to the Theology of
Marcella Althaus-Reid

Thia Cooper

scm press

© Thia Cooper 2021

Published in 2021 by SCM Press
Editorial office
3rd Floor, Invicta House,
108–114 Golden Lane,
London EC1Y 0TG, UK
www.scmpress.co.uk

SCM Press is an imprint of Hymns Ancient & Modern Ltd
(a registered charity)

Hymns Ancient & Modern® is a registered trademark of
Hymns Ancient & Modern Ltd
13A Hellesdon Park Road, Norwich,
Norfolk NR6 5DR, UK

British Library Cataloguing in Publication data
A catalogue record for this book is available
from the British Library

978-0-334-06162-5

Typeset by Regent Typesetting

Contents

Acknowledgements

First, I acknowledge my friend Andrew Foster Davis, a Methodist pastor. Over coffee, we were talking about Marcella's work and how fascinating but difficult it could be to fully understand. I said I should write an article summarizing her key themes and he replied, 'I think that would be a book.' And he was right. Second, I want to thank my assistant Anna LoFaro for all her editing and reference help. All remaining mistakes are mine but she made sure there were as few as possible. Third, of course, I acknowledge Marcella and the huge influence she has had on my life and theology. I am grateful to her for helping me to navigate the harms of Christian theology and to imagine alternatives. Fourth, I want to thank David Shervington for engaging SCM Press in this process and fully supporting my efforts, which were, of course, derailed by Covid-19. And finally, I want to thank my friends and family for all their support and love, especially Raoul.

Introduction

> Based on sexual categories and heterosexual binary systems, obsessed with sexual behaviour and orders, every theological discourse is implicitly sexual. (Althaus-Reid, 2000c, p. 22)

Marcella Althaus-Reid's work was groundbreaking and prophetic and remains forward-thinking more than a decade after her death. She began her theological trajectory by critiquing Latin American liberation theology for failing to follow its own method, and feminist theologies for remaining within a gender analysis and forgetting to focus on the lives of real women. She searched for the sacred in the female and in the indigenous, using a post-colonial and sexual analysis. She crafted a new theology, which she called 'indecent'. She pushed forward the boundaries of talking about sex and theology and urged us to continue this work. She did consider herself a feminist and liberation theologian. However, she expanded beyond these formal frameworks to work in indecent and queer theologies. For Althaus-Reid, theology has both ignored and denigrated sex. Instead, we can talk about and celebrate sex as a way to know God.

> Our task and our joy is to find or simply recognize God sitting amongst us, at any time, in any gay bar or in the home of a camp friend who decorates her living room as a chapel and doesn't leave her rosary at home when going to a salsa bar. (Althaus-Reid, 2003c, p. 4)

Althaus-Reid wanted to understand how we relate to God through sexual experiences and particularly in sexual experiences marginalized by society and traditional theology (totalitarian theology, T-theology, as she shortened it). This book aims to introduce how Althaus-Reid indecented and queered Christian theology in her search for God.

For Althaus-Reid, although traditional theology tries to avoid sex, it constantly considers sex, usually negatively. Theologies have argued that a heterosexual marriage is the only appropriate context for sex and anything else separates us from God. Rather than stay within the centre that marginalizes so many people, Althaus-Reid argued that God is found at the margins of society. In fact, God is a marginal God, emerging from and living with the marginalized. To find God requires breaking out of the formalized Western straitjacket of theology. To see beyond what we have been taught is difficult and requires analysis from our realities. Helpful in this regard are academic subjects such as post-colonialism, gender and sexuality studies, and critiques of capitalism. For Althaus-Reid,

> We can think theologically at the intersection of postmodernism, the expansion of capitalism in globalization processes and in the critical stand of the construction of the sexual body which comes from post-colonial and Queer Theology ... What we find here is the presence of systems made up of a combination of different kinds of exchanges and transgressions, which do not need to be equivalent amongst themselves while forming a topography of eros. (Althaus-Reid, 2003c, p. 30)

The goal is to deconstruct any hegemonic framework and enable alternatives to flourish, expanding the narrow confines traditional Christianity allowed God, celebrating eros as well as agape in all their diversity.

Althaus-Reid chose to articulate an indecent theology deliberately in contrast to the requirement of 'decency', which oppressed so many people. Decency oppressed women in particular, with its dress and behaviour codes, which constrained and confined women, in society and in theology.

Indecent Theology is a book on Sexual Political Theology intended as a critical continuation of Feminist Liberation

Theology using a multidisciplinary approach and drawing on Sexual Theory (Butler; Sedgwick; Garber), Postcolonial criticism (Fanon, Cabral, Said), Queer studies and theologies (Stuart; Goss; Weeks; Daly), Marxist studies (Laclau and Mouffe; Dussel), Continental Philosophy (Derrida; Deleuze and Guattari; Baudrillard) and Systematic Theology. (Althaus-Reid, 2000c, p. 7)

Beginning from feminist liberation theology, she delved deeply into a variety of academic subjects to better reflect the realities of the poorest and most marginalized, whose ways of living and loving are outside traditional constructs. Her expertise spanned post-colonialism, philosophy, queer studies, and theology. Where many of these areas of study have taken strides in considering the excluded, in moving beyond binaries, systematic theology has not.

Althaus-Reid's work can seem difficult to fully comprehend, spanning as many areas as it does. However, there are several key themes that surface and resurface in her work, which can guide the reader through the more complicated material. This book aims to provide an overview of these key themes and introduce the reader to further readings on these themes. One does not have to be an expert in any particular subject to read Althaus-Reid's work, but it is helpful to enter the conversation with an open mind. Theology, for liberationists and for Althaus-Reid, is not limited to the study of Christianity; it encompasses all of our life experiences and academic knowledge.

First and foremost, she did not aim to produce a systematic theology but instead to highlight theologies from the margins. With this work, she followed the earliest liberationists.

From the beginning, the aim was not to reproduce a systematic theology from a Latin American perspective but *to do* theology. It was said that a letter written by a community demanding one tap for clean water in a neighbourhood had more value than a book on dogmatics. (Althaus-Reid, 1996c, p. 387)

She criticized the later development of liberation theology, which preferred to formalize itself, becoming acceptable in Western academia rather than remaining faithful to the margins. Theology, for Althaus-Reid, should emerge from the experience of real people in all their diversity.

To be clear, we should judge any theme from Althaus-Reid's work in the light of the reality of the most marginalized. As Althaus-Reid herself wrote, the following characteristics are crucial to doing theology:

1 *Non-neutrality.* No theology is neutral. 'Every theology is ideologically biased and supports a social configuration of the world and political structures ... By making them [presuppositions] public, they open themselves to dialogue with different perspectives and experiences' (Althaus-Reid, 1996c, p. 388). Every theology works from particular assumptions and frameworks; being honest about these means one can then assess not only the theology but the systems it supports. Neutrality is impossible because it inherently supports the status quo. It may be passive but it is still enabling. Althaus-Reid worked to unearth the hidden but dominant sexual framework of traditional theologies.

2 *Option for the poor.* Theology should always prioritize the marginalized. 'In Latin America, the situation of chronic poverty, social injustice, and political dependency has provided the local for theological reflection ... The Bible shows the poorest of the poor as God's favoured people' (Althaus-Reid, 1996c, p. 388). The majority of people in Latin America live in economic, political and other forms of poverty. As Jesus and God have throughout the biblical texts, theology should side with the poor. In particular, Althaus-Reid emphasized those completely excluded from society. Theology should reflect the excluded's perspectives.

3 *The concept of 'realidad'.* Theology should focus on reality rather than ideology. '*La realidad* implies not only a reflection upon the actual circumstances in which we are living but also an analysis of the historical causes of those circumstances' (Althaus-Reid, 1996c, p. 388). Realities can be

'constructed' by those in power and may not reflect the situation on the ground. Theologies have constructed 'realities' too and need to rectify this problem. For Althaus-Reid, this reflection on reality begins with bodies, in particular the bodies of women and the excluded.

4 *Praxis.* Theology is more than pondering; it is also what we do that determines our theology. 'This refers to the process of action and reflection that operates in this way of doing theology' (Althaus-Reid, 1996c, p. 388). It is not enough to think; we also must act. Any theology must include action. A theology is judged by its actions and effects, not its thought.

5 *Orthopraxis.* Theology should not be trying to find the correct ideology or rule to follow; it should be aiming for better practices, towards justice. 'In liberation theology the reflection is first of all upon the world, and only then is it considered how God has manifested Godself in the historical events of humankind's liberation. This process is known as second-act theology' (Althaus-Reid, 1996c, p. 388). First one examines reality and then one examines God. The goal is not to find the right rules but practices to try, which then require further reflection. Hence, life experience and theology speak back and forth to each other, with life experience shaping and correcting when theology falls into ideals or ideologies.

6 *Structures of sin.* Where traditional theologies have focused on the sins and salvation of individuals, it is important to address the sin and oppression that exists within structures. 'Without denying the reality of individual sin, liberation theology concentrates on the structural aspects of sin, that is the macro-structures that perpetuate social injustice, poverty, and violence around the world' (Althaus-Reid, 1996c, p. 388). In particular, Althaus-Reid examined structures of heterosexuality, patriarchy and capitalism that cause harm. Our dominant systems include sin; we need to change these structures.

This book addresses 11 themes present in Marcella's work:

1 The theological marketplace in which we teach, research and act.
2 The hermeneutical circle, liberation theology's method.
3 Post-colonialism's importance to help undo theology's harms.
4 Capitalism and the need to prioritize the excluded.
5 The importance of women and woman-God to theology.
6 The body, as the starting point for doing theology.
7 Indecency as a way to expand theology.
8 Heterosexuality as the harmful basis of traditional theologies.
9 Queering as a way to undo the harm and build alternatives.
10 The marginal God as the broader understanding of a God out of the closet.
11 Crucifixions/resurrections, so badly needed to change our world and work toward justice.

I also begin with a brief biography of Marcella to share a little context for her work. Finally, I suggest starting points for engaging each theme, located at the end of each chapter.

Many people have wrestled with her work over the past two decades and I hope this introductory book will expand her reach even further, as we follow her in the search for God and a world of loving justice.

I

Biography

I am a sexual theologian, a postfeminist, and more than that, a queer and political theologian of liberation. (Althaus-Reid, 2011, p. 451)

Marcella Althaus-Reid combined being intensely private with sharing stories of her life in her work. Here, I want to provide a bit of context, to share her setting and some of the political and economic situations she encountered. I do not, however, state that this context is 'why' her work is the way that it is but knowing a writer's setting helps us to see what may have influenced her thinking. Many of us who knew Marcella have diverse stories to share, each a piece of Marcella's life but by no means the whole.

Marcella was an only child, born in Rosario, Argentina in 1952 to Alberto and Ada Althaus. She was born into Peron's government, growing up in tumultuous political and economic times, including several coup d'etats and the 1976–83 dictatorship and Dirty War. As a child, her neighbourhood was bombed. As a teenager, she and her family were evicted from their housing. She told me that when she was a bit older, she remembered going to bed looking forward to buying a chicken the next day with the money she'd earned that day. However, when she went out to shop the next morning, she found inflation had risen so sharply overnight the chicken was ten times more expensive than the day before; she could not afford it. Life was unstable and challenging.

The religious environment was also challenging. She was born into the Catholic tradition and wanted to become a minister but was repeatedly discouraged, told that women were not supposed to attend seminary. As a teenager, she gravitated towards Methodism, a denomination in which women could be ordained. Finally, she was able to pursue a degree in theology at ISEDET (Instituto Superior Evangelico de Estudios Teologicos), a Methodist institute vibrant with liberation theologians, and a dangerous place to be during the dictatorship. As part of her degree she worked with base communities and learned from several of the first generation of liberation theologians like José Miguez Bonino[1] and José Severino Croatto.[2] She told me about inviting homeless people into a church in Buenos Aires to talk about life and God, over cigarettes and alcohol, and of course being criticized by others for her actions. But shouldn't a church be a space for anyone to talk about life and God?

While at ISEDET, she travelled to Norway for a Christian student programme. There she met Gordon Reid, from Scotland, whom she later married. She settled in Scotland, working in communities of poor women in Dundee and Perth. She then pursued and completed a PhD at the University of St Andrews in the early 1990s on the subject of Paul Ricoeur[3] and liberation theology's method.

She attended Quaker services in the UK and became deeply involved with the Metropolitan Community Church. She told me that she was frustrated attending a Protestant church where the congregation had to be silent, except for ritual formal responses. She wanted to speak aloud when the spirit moved her. Once, in her University of Edinburgh office, I commented on a photo of her smiling broadly in a church. She laughed and told me that the whole scenario ended quite quickly as the priest realized who she was and chased her out of the church yelling at her. She had her fair share of critiques and criticism, as a quick search of the web will show you. One of her colleagues told me her theology was 'primitive', which seemed ironic as I first made my way through *Indecent Theology*.

The University of Edinburgh hired her to teach, on a one-year contract, and after several renewals and promotions she was given a chair in Contextual Theology. Althaus-Reid was the first woman to hold a chair in the School of Divinity. At

Edinburgh, she directed the MTh in theology, culture and development, mentored several PhD students, and taught a variety of classes and sessions on liberation theologies. As her PhD student, I remember leaving a meeting with her feeling great because she had pointed out a paragraph in my draft chapter that she said 'got to the heart of what I wanted to say'. It was only much later that I realized her comment meant the remaining 20 pages did not! In my experience, she was supportive but engagingly critical, which helped me deepen my thinking and practice.

As for some personal titbits, Marcella loved shoes (especially boots) and Frida Kahlo.[4] And when in meetings, you knew when she started using her hand fan briskly that she was about to weigh in. Finally, Marcella was tirelessly kind but quick to respond, defend and protect others when they were being denigrated. One example of her attention to the marginalization of others comes from her chapter on Mark. Robert Goss[5] told the story of asking Marcella about the dedication to this chapter, which was to 'RG'. Her response was, 'I envision you as the unemployed Jesus. I wrote about the figure of Jesus in Mark's Gospel with you and the tenure battle at Webster in mind' (Shore-Goss, 2010, p. 10). Goss had been denied tenure, and Marcella and others vociferously condemned this denial. André Musskopf[6] also tells of Marcella's insistence every time they met to send her some of his writing. 'We Latin Americans have to stick together, help each other ... send me something you wrote, so I can publish it' (Musskopf, 2010, p. 229). Many of us were supported by and defended by Marcella at various points in our lives.

She belonged to a 'collocation,' as she called it, of women and people of varying sexualities from around the globe, working in community towards justice. During her career, she wrote three books and more than 40 chapters and articles in Spanish and English. She was invited to speak and teach all over the world, including Brazil, New Zealand and the USA. She died, aged 56, after a lengthy battle with cancer.

Notes

1 José Miguez Bonino (1924–2012) was an Argentinian Methodist liberation theologian.

2 José Severino Croatto (1930–2004) was an Argentinian Catholic liberation theologian and Hebrew Bible scholar.

3 Paul Ricoeur (1913–2005) was a French philosopher, who engaged phenomenology (how we experience) and hermeneutics (how we interpret).

4 Frida Kahlo (1907–53) was a Mexican artist, who specialized in painting self-portraits.

5 Robert Goss (1948–) is a gay theologian and pastor.

6 André Musskopf is a Brazilian Lutheran theologian, denied ordination by the ELCA (Evangelical Lutheran Church) in Brazil.

2

The Theological Marketplace: Activism, Teaching, Scholarship

Althaus-Reid was clear that activism should be the starting point for scholarship and that action should be integrated into the classroom. Separating action from reflection leads to an ineffective action or a disconnected ideology. She also critiqued the marketplace of academia, which limits effective theologizing. Action is key to liberation theology. One has to put this thinking into practice; thinking alone does not produce theology. Althaus-Reid recognized that being an activist-scholar is difficult in the capitalist system. It requires teaching against the grain, researching against the grain and acting against the grain. Since liberation theology should emerge from practice, as the next chapter explores, one needs room to practise and participate in community in order to craft and teach liberation theologies.

Althaus-Reid followed in the steps of Paulo Freire, arguing for a liberating form of education, one that opens a student's eyes to the world and its systems.

> The content and the style of education are neither neutral nor passive elements, but powerful ideological contributors to the lives of our societies ... Freire developed a style of work called 'education for liberation' which involved dialoguing with adult people ... The key was that the poor and marginalized of our societies should learn to interrogate and discover the mechanisms of oppression which has rendered them as excluded from society. (Althaus-Reid, 2006a, p. 1)

Education is not neutral; it comes from a particular perspective and has specific aims. The aim of liberation pedagogy is to show how things have come to be, how what is seen as normal can be challenged, to enable us to gain the tools to act. Our teaching today should be focused on opening our students' eyes to structures of power. We also need to work with the poorest and most marginalized in our own societies; people outside our universities or colleges. Hence, our work with marginalized communities tends to take place outside working hours.

When Althaus-Reid arrived in Scotland she worked in a poor community with women, beginning conversations and opening dialogue with the issues that affected their daily lives. She described in detail one such conversation, continuing for weeks, around issues of cleaning, dirt, salvation and sin. After seeing a billboard for detergent on a walk together,

> We spoke about obsessive cleansing behaviour, and everybody shared a story which linked cleansing to a religious experience which did not fit our real lives ... We are living at a time in which globalization processes have taken poverty to a new dimension of social exclusion, while our whole environment suffers under the weight of humankind's own greediness and disrespect for life. (Althaus-Reid, 2006a, pp. 2–3)

These women saw an overemphasis on cleanliness in life in general and in religion, a rejection and exclusion of things and people seen to be dirty. Like this example, we need to learn and teach about the connections between our daily lives and global issues. The university system needs to make room for such teaching and learning, both inside and outside university walls.

Teaching Theology Requires Dissent and Action

First, teaching theology as a liberationist feminist requires dissent because the current system prioritizes teaching in predetermined frameworks. 'Theology' is taught as systematic, and sometimes denominational, prioritizing but not naming

European male theology. For Althaus-Reid, it has a military feel. 'I deliberately use a military metaphor because it explains the whole ethos of the process of current teaching of theology I want to avoid. Military training implies a process of discipline and homogenization' (Althaus-Reid, 1996b, p. 134). Sometimes teaching theology appears to be introducing students to the correct systematic theology. Instead, teaching should be directly related to the diverse daily lives of people, not only in the classroom but outside the university, enabling students and others to craft their own theologies, their own thinking about God. 'This way of doing and teaching theology will make obsolete the current alienation between academia and the community, and between feminist theology as research and the daily life of the women in our cities' (Althaus-Reid, 1996b, p. 134). Teaching and research should enable us and our students to connect with and reflect on what they see in their own daily lives, particularly when it comes to issues of liberation.

Shifting our way of teaching is difficult within the Western academic context. Althaus-Reid stated, 'I usually start my courses on Liberation Theology explaining to my students that this theology needs to be taught in a different way' (Althaus-Reid, 1996a, p. 75). Lecturing on liberation is oxymoronic. Further, theologies of liberation require reflection on subjects outside of theology, such as economics, politics, anthropology and sociology. When she studied in Argentina, she noted, 'every week we have a "group therapy" session to know more about each other in community, and theology was part of a multidisciplinary curriculum ... Our exams were mostly oral, and in groups: students needed to learn to work together' (Althaus-Reid, 1996a, p. 75). If liberation theology is to be community theology then it should be examined and crafted in community. Hence, we need to connect our teaching to daily life in community. Instead, our academic system is focused on the individual, for example, our grading system is not communal. Each student receives an individual grade, an individual degree.

Second, teaching feminist and liberation theologies requires dissent from the framework that labels such theologies as 'contextual'. Theology remains the realm of older, white, straight, Christian males parading in a European line of history, and anything outside of this frame receives the label of 'x theology' or 'x theologian'. A course on theology and race, sex and/or class gets a special label. In European institutions, according to Althaus-Reid, 'difference is incorporated into the teaching system as "different", *exo*, "from another place", as a sort of touristic attraction deprived of the power of articulation of a new theological discourse which could radically challenge the Western white and male discourse' (Althaus-Reid, 1996a, p. 71). Our courses in liberation and feminisms have a niche alongside the main model of teaching theology, as a sideshow attraction. These courses do not disturb the core teaching or framework of academic theology. However, this framework is patriarchal, Western-centric and narrow. Any theology implicitly includes issues of race, sex, and so forth; however, these issues are ignored.

Third, key to liberation theology is action, which the academy ignores and devalues. 'With few exceptions ... the universities have a system which discourages any type of dialogue except with fellow theologians' (Althaus-Reid, 1996b, p. 135). Any activism has to be done outside the boundaries of one's formal career or teaching. Yet, liberation theology should be interdisciplinary and issue-based. To find the issues one needs to be in community. 'When I started my first degree in theology in ISEDET, Buenos Aires, I went to work in a base community as part of the academic curriculum of the seminary' (Althaus-Reid, 1996b, p. 137). For Althaus-Reid, working in community was part of academic learning. In the USA, it is occasionally possible to incorporate a service-learning component into smaller classes, however, the practice is exceptional rather than the norm. Theology is not supposed to be solely God-talk, 'the point is that I miss theology as "God-walk"' (Althaus-Reid, 1996a, p. 76). How are we to learn about God without doing? How are we to test our theology without real-world engagement?

We cannot do theology from the marginalized if we do not interact with the marginalized. This lack of community engagement is a particular paradox of higher education. Althaus-Reid asked, 'How can we reflect theologically (and, especially, ethically) on issues of exclusion when Third World students are excluded not only by ridiculously high fees, but by the insistence on accepting only Western patterns of argument, evaluation and assessment?' (Althaus-Reid, 2004c, p. 379). The aims of liberation and our 'closed' university systems contradict each other. Even when we invite underrepresented students into our college and classrooms we expect them to fit in rather than changing ourselves to meet their needs. For the marginalized in our classrooms, we need to stop teaching them from the centre. Further, if the marginalized are not in our classrooms, we need to find ways to connect with them.

Teaching theology is not about disseminating previously accepted knowledge; it is about crafting knowledge and action together to change systems and structures, to build an understanding of God together. Althaus-Reid stated: 'The theology of God *acompaña* starts at the point of affirming that those women can articulate a theological discourse of change in their lives, a theosocial discourse' (Althaus-Reid, 1996a, p. 73). Theology should begin with reality, understanding that each of us has experience of knowing God. God accompanies women throughout their lives. These experiences should continually change, challenge and expand theology. Instead, Althaus-Reid asked, 'Has Feminist Theology become decent?' (Althaus-Reid, 1996a, p. 73). If feminist and liberation theologies are taught without real-world connections, they are neither feminist nor liberationist.

Scholarship Requires Community Engagement

Our scholarship should also connect to daily life, again difficult to achieve in the academic tenure and promotion system. 'In Britain, the university has a strong censorship role on community engagement. A faculty of divinity may censor any engagement with a community through the allocation of hours of work and duties to be carried out outside working hours'

(Althaus-Reid, p. 2004c). While not prohibited, community work is not considered part of the formal work of the teacher-scholar. Instead, research and scholarship are guided by university requirements. 'This includes, for instance, research, when done for the economic benefit of the university, using the timescale and the output (publication) of the sort that is valuable for the university' (Althaus-Reid, 2004c, p. 378). Publishing in peer-reviewed academic journals and with academic publishers is valued. Materials aimed at people outside university walls are devalued. Publishing for non-academics, the people who make up the majority of the world, and certainly the vast majority of the excluded, is not counted as academic scholarship.

This censorship is exacerbated by the lack of tenure-track and tenured positions, which keeps us from forming community. It takes time and community to work towards justice, time to build trust with and become part of a community. 'Short, unstable contracts ... have forced teachers to move from place to place searching for jobs or promotion (equivalent to salary increases in the present circumstances), thus disconnecting themselves from any long-term engagement with a geographical community' (Althaus-Reid, 2004c, p. 378). If a liberationist is moving from region to region, community engagement and building trust in a particular community becomes difficult. Commitment to community is eroded by the need to move to secure a job. We are constantly uprooted.

The Academic Marketplace Excludes Activism

If and when a tenure-track job is secured, one has to continue to work within the system to achieve tenure or promotion.

> Everything plays a role in these structures of sin, and a system of promotions which are obtainable through the pursuit not of community work, but of more administrative work and publications, makes clear which values a theologian should expect to be respected. (Althaus-Reid, 2004c, p. 378)

Again, the goals of liberation and a career in theology contradict each other. Without outright banning, a university can constrain what is taught and researched. 'Censorship also works simply by failing to provide the necessary conditions for developing any alternative praxis' (Althaus-Reid, 2004c, p. 379). Most universities do not provide resources for us to research and teach outside normative frameworks. Althaus-Reid wanted to make clear that liberationists work within sinful structures of colonialism, capitalism, patriarchy and heterosexuality, even when trying to struggle against them.

The theologian needs to recognize their own situation within the capitalist marketplace, among other structures. Being a theologian, a theology professor, is a job within the capitalist system. 'It is with our theological production that we have entered and become fully participants in the economic structure of society' (Althaus-Reid, 2004c, p. 376). Producing and consuming theology has become part of the capitalist system. Our work as theologians either fits into the capitalist system or is dismissed by that system, in which case we may lose our jobs. As liberationist teacher-scholars most of our work is unpaid. 'Many of us ... are ... thinking and writing in the hours which follow work, understanding work as the long hours of teaching and ever-increasing administrative duties which exceed the normal working day and go unpaid and unrecognized' (Althaus-Reid, 2004c, p. 377). What we teach and what we research and what we publish are increasingly constrained by what the university system considers appropriate teaching, research and scholarship, and that is determined by the marketplace. At college and university, students are the consumers and we teach what they will buy; publishers publish what the largest number of people will buy.

The theologian as worker is kept from producing an activist theology. Further, when theology is published, it is alienated from the producer, the theologian who wrote the work and the people who initially lived the theology. Liberation theologies emerge from communities of the marginalized, focused on praxis. However, theologies become formalized and separated from these communities. Alienation continues. Our work as theologians is a form of exploited and exploitative labour.

Achieving some stability in one's career, a permanent job, is antithetical to the concept of liberation itself, yet important to survival. Success is achieved off the stories of the oppressed. Althaus-Reid noted that horrific experiences like the Holocaust and the Rwandan genocide have spawned many books, with good intentions, but still profiting from disaster (Althaus-Reid, 2000c, p. 27). It is important to tell stories to change systems but the goal is not individual success, which makes it difficult to work within the capitalist system. The theology of liberation emerges from the oppressed but, if produced and published, it becomes a marker of an individual's success rather than a continuing community dialogue. Althaus-Reid argued that

> the laws of market production apply to theological production. For instance: 1. *The law of reversal*: The more the worker produces, the less the worker consumes, means in this context that theology is a surplus value of human suffering. It alienates by taking possession, extorting from others what belongs to them. (Althaus-Reid, 2000c, p. 27)

The first stage is that writing and publishing formal theology takes it away from the producer/the worker, the community living out the theology. Writing down theology makes it the theologian's property. Second is '*The law of ownership*: The suffering poor provide in this process we are describing, creativity and questioning of theological relevance, but they do not own the means to produce their discourse, neither the end product ... of their labour power' (Althaus-Reid, 2000c, p. 28). The poor do not decide whether or not to publish, or what to publish. Once the theology is written and sold in the marketplace, it no longer belongs to the poor, no matter the good intentions of the theologians. In this sense, as liberation theology became formalized it moved further away from the community of the poor. What we write tends to be taken as the set reality, rather than as a moment in an ongoing process of action and reflection, available to all communities.

It is difficult to find a tenure-track position, achieve tenure and remain an activist-teacher. The university and marketplace, key markers in capitalist society, devalue activist theology. Althaus-Reid critiqued the 'need to produce theology as a consumer good' (Althaus-Reid, 2004b, p. 107). Both the Christian church and the university system fit well within the capitalist model. The success of a theologian or a church is based on how many books are read, how many people attend the church. Yet, theology is to bring people closer to God in thought and action. Liberation theology was not about marketable success. The idea was to change people's lives, not fill the churches. How can we achieve this goal?

Towards the end of the previous century, liberation theology declined in the marketplace, declared dead by many. Communities of the poor, however, continued to do theology; it was simply no longer marketable in Europe and the USA. Initially, liberation theology achieved success by challenging traditional theology in some senses. However, liberation theology disconnected from both the established church and, later, the poorest. Liberation theology instead adapted to the marketplace.

> The Western theological market took that very important first attempt at a Liberation Theology in search of its subject and methodology and forced it to become marketable and decent ... Cultural Liberation Theology was relaunched, leaving the political and economical analysis aside. (Althaus-Reid, 2000c, p. 31)

Some liberation theologians focused more on publishing for the US and European markets than on doing theology in community. Latin American liberation theology's radicalness was tamed, becoming an example of cultural analysis rather than challenging theology itself. Those of us working in the area of liberation need to recognize this disconnect. It is easy to choose decency to gain a stable career and notoriety. It is easy to support the system to protect our small gains.

For Althaus-Reid, it is important for liberationist scholar-activists to create community among themselves, to support each other in the struggle towards justice.

A movement provides us with several things:

1 The possibility of organizing flexible structures of community work according to need, and disposing of them when obsolete, while retaining a feeling of continuation. [Crafting a broad network means we can retain community, even when organizations shift and change.]

2 The ability to be in tune with the *Kairos* in its different facets and challenges, working at different levels but with a feeling of unity. [A broad movement enables us to bring together diverse actions and react quickly to new challenges.]

3 The teaching of a new understanding of the role of the feminist theologian; the rediscovery of her prophetic vocation for transformation, supported by other people who do not objectify her in relation to patriarchal categories of importance. [A movement connects activist-scholars to the real world and to each other.]

4 Basic support and encouragement from women sharing the same 'indecent' visions, avoiding fragmentation through work done in solidarity. [And a movement enables us, particularly women, not to be alone in the struggle. Although academia treats us as individuals, we can support each other in community. The stronger our networks, the more we can engage with communities even when location or life changes. Being in community can also help us realize that we are not the 'strange' ones; it is the system that is constraining inappropriately.] (Althaus-Reid, 1996b, p. 138)

It is only through working together that we can enact change. Inherently, liberation theologians should not care about selling books or filling churches but about ending oppression. As liberationists, we need neither formal theology nor the church hierarchy. With the '"second coming of the Spirit" ... then the Church will not need theology neither vice-versa, but people defining needs and relationships in their own terms and from the margins' (Althaus-Reid, 2004b, p. 112). Rather than receiving our theology from a patriarchal, hierarchical church, the Spirit enables us to craft theologies together in community. This crafting requires us to work outside the system and against the system.

Suggested reading

Althaus-Reid, M., 1996a, 'Both Indecent and Ex-centric: Teaching Feminist Theology for Articulation or for Exoticism?', in Althaus-Reid, M., ed., *Liberating the Vision: Papers of the Summer School 24th–28th May*, pp. 71–7, Southampton: Centre for Contemporary Theology, LSU.

Althaus-Reid, M., 1996b., 'The Indecency of Her Teaching: Notes for Cuceb Teaching of Feminist Theology in Europe', in Fiorenza, E. S. and M. S. Copeland, eds, *Feminist Theology in Different Contexts*, pp. 133–40, London: SCM Press.

Althaus-Reid, M., 2004b, 'Does the Church Need Theology or Vice Versa? A Materialist Analysis Concerning the Current Theological Industry and its Church Market', in Althaus-Reid, M., *From Feminist Theology to Indecent Theology*, pp. 124–42, London: SCM Press.

3

The Hermeneutical Circle

Key to liberation theology is its method, which became known as the hermeneutical (interpretive) circle. In its simplest form, it is 'see–judge–act'. However, each stage has important pieces and Althaus-Reid critiqued the shortcuts that many theologians take, leading to theology being stunted or repressed before it can even be expressed in thought, words and actions. She began her critique with her PhD, which analysed Ricoeur, several liberation theologians, and how communities in Latin America actually used the hermeneutical circle. She continued thereafter to criticize liberation theology for failing to implement its method. Rather than continuing the circle, some theologians took one expression of theology as central, narrowing the possibilities.

The Importance of the Marginalized and the Problems with Traditional Interpretation

Colonization brought Christianity to the Americas. Europeans assumed their version of Christianity with its European framework was the correct and only version. The indigenous were not allowed input into the creation of new Christianities or allowed to adapt Christianity into indigenous traditions. Christianity and civilization went together, according to the Europeans. Indigenous traditions and un-civilization did too. For Althaus-Reid, 'The reason why the Latin American cultural ethos has suffered a process of disintegration and assimilation, has been the profound identification established between the Christian faith, and a specific external model of culture and civilization' (Althaus-Reid, 1993, p. 341). Latin American culture had to submit to European Christianity, losing its own history and culture. What Ricoeur's method enabled, according to Althaus-Reid, was a process of truly seeing reality, reading the Bible anew, enabling Latin Americans to undo the Europeanization of the text and reality. Latin Americans could read through their own lenses.

Key to the hermeneutical circle is to ensure that the poorest and most marginalized are heard and their readings prioritized. Instead, 'Biblical interpretation in Latin America has had five hundred years of cooperating actively with the ideological system which has kept the continent in a chronic state of underdevelopment of its own possibilities' (Althaus-Reid, 1993, p. 373). Historical biblical interpretations were always produced by European authorities. The readings of the poorest may stand in dramatic contrast and should be the focus of theologies.

> We can say that for the poor, 'to find themselves in the Scriptures' means that they need to find the alterity, and the different meanings that do not necessarily result in contradiction ... because the identity of the text is constituted by that which defies the permanence of the same. Canaanizing biblical interpretation is then to accept and welcome the irruption of the alterity in the text, and to open up a dialogue where the criterion for truth could come from a dialogue where the experience of Israel could be understood in its possibility of experiencing the different, or in an aesthetic experience of otherness. (Althaus-Reid, 1993, pp. 375–6)

Latin Americans need to dialogue with the text, not just accept the dominant reading. Throughout her work, Althaus-Reid referred to a Canaanite perspective, reading the texts from below, thinking about how the Israelites could have behaved differently when they encountered others. Alternative readings from varying perspectives can talk and work together. Other understandings of the text may differ but not necessarily contradict. No community reading should be rejected or excluded because each helps us to understand more fully the varying contexts and to build a more holistic picture.

The inclusion of the poorest and most marginalized in the hermeneutical circle is key to figuring out whether Christianity is relevant for Latin Americans, particularly the indigenous groups denigrated and destroyed by the Europeans.

> The Guarani people use the same term for 'word' and 'soul'. We can say then that Latin Americans lost their soul (religious experience) and word (language) at the same time. Only what we have called a process of Canaanization could make the pobres readers and writers of their own biblical text. (Althaus-Reid, 1993, p. 377)

The indigenous were offered Christianity but they had to reject life and culture as they knew it. Recovering varied Latin American perspectives began in the base ecclesial communities,[1] which were the starting point for liberation theologies, prominent in the 1970s. Reading the Bible from the 'underside of history' produces different meanings. Reading the text as a Canaanite gives a completely different perspective to that of an Israelite and opens the text to new questions.

Reading in Community

Communities come together to read the Bible, bringing different perspectives to create active theologies. Althaus-Reid highlighted the importance of the base communities for the crafting of the hermeneutical circle in practice and thus emerging liberation theologies.

> Labour, work and action, three elements which Ricoeur considers important in the disclosure of the 'I' who interprets, are present and 'alive' in the interpretative community of the CEBs. These communities turn the 'I' into the 'We'. The BECs show the 'We' of the Latin American pueblo who, interpreting its life and faith ... does an effective poiesis of social transformation. (Althaus-Reid, 1993, p. 399)

Rather than read individually, the BECs read in community, analysed in community and acted in community. This 'we' can change Christianity and society through the process of the hermeneutical circle. Liberation theology's method happens in community.

The Hermeneutical Circle

The hermeneutical circle is described as having three or four steps, depending on how the middle stage is separated out.

As Althaus-Reid explained, the first step is for the community to read life. 'Starting with the concept of the community as interpreter and interpreted, the methodology of conscientization is used at this stage to "decode" structures of oppression that have been internalized and remain unchallenged, often because of theological concepts such as resignation' (Althaus-Reid, 1996c, p. 388). Conscientization means to become aware of the world and its systems. Conscientization helps us to resist the harmful theology that tells us to submit rather than resist structures of power. The community begins to understand their situation in a broader context. They ask, why are we poor, marginalized and excluded?

We need to see reality as it is, not just as we have been told. Seeing is very difficult. It requires us to examine reality in detail, picking out the elements that we normally absorb without noticing. The poor and excluded have a clear suspicion of the 'normal' systems, which have rejected them.

> The theme of the 'option for the poor' is a contribution to the search for a mythical nucleus of Latin America ... Only by a rediscovering of the symbolic universe of the continent can the process of liberation and freedom be accomplished. (Althaus-Reid, 1996c, p. 354)

Starting with the poor enables them to define themselves and decide how to act. For Althaus-Reid, the core of a community's being comes from its own history and experiences, not the history of others. A post-colonial analysis helps us understand this distinction, as we address in Chapter 5.

The second step in the hermeneutical circle is to judge, analysing from our knowledge and the biblical text. Sometimes judging is broken into two steps:

(a) Setting life and Scripture side by side. 'This is a moment of analysis where liberation theology uses social sciences and political theory ... The community discussion of key issues in their lives, together with a reading of the bible that liberated the text from the constraints of orthodoxy, becoming closer to an orthopraxis, transformed biblical exegesis' (Althaus-Reid, 1996c, p. 389). Understanding the world, the poor then read life and the text side by side; life and the text each help to analyse the other. Neither is prioritized over the other.

(b) Then the community critiques Scripture. 'Understanding the text in community[:] This is the moment in the process of the hermeneutical circle when the text becomes part of the historical experience of the community reading it' (Althaus-Reid, 1996c, p. 389). The community's lives and the text then merge, producing a new interpretation of both life and the text. The text is not closed; new interpretations continue to emerge today.

How the Bible is read differs with differing experiences, which is why it is critical to read with those normally marginalized and excluded. For example, Althaus-Reid, in the context of the Lazarus story from John 11, states:

> Only a man whose life experience had been made up of ruptures from and departures of lovers, in the tension of keeping the heterosexual masked ball going, in his job and family, is able to see a dramatic love story between Jesus and his intimate friend. (Althaus-Reid, 2000c, p. 129)

A gay man may see love in the text that another person might miss. Our life experiences lead us to see different aspects of the text, helping to build a fuller understanding in community.

Theologians like Beatriz Melano Couch[2] also helped to adapt Ricoeur's 'Quadrilateral Model' for biblical interpretation in a Latin American context and emphasized the following:

1 the non-neutrality of the methods of interpretation.
2 the limitations of his/her chosen methodology. (Althaus-Reid, 1993, p. 186)

Reading is not neutral; we come with our own questions, our own perspectives and our own blind spots. We need to recognize differing starting points and experiences as valid but not universal. This recognition is particularly important for historical interpretations, which often ignored both aspects.

Various liberation theologians also distinguished the freedom of these readings from traditional interpretation. For example, Croatto argued for 'sintonia' rather than 'concordismo'. Althaus-Reid defined concordismo as 'the abuse of the historical readings of the Scripture, and the closure of the meaning of the text from the perspective of the original sense (if such a thing could be recovered)' (Althaus-Reid, 1993, p. 366). In some traditional hermeneutics, only one interpretation is considered valid; the text is fixed and closed. Sintonia, in contrast, is the '"tuning in" of the Scriptures with their reality' (Althaus-Reid, 1993, p. 297). New meaning can come from the biblical text and so interpretation should continue. The reader is part of the historical community of readers but remains questioning and critical and open to inspiration for new interpretations.

> The effects (or actions) of liberation of the Bible are rescued by Croatto through the use of historical criticism, and the category of pueblo pobre (the poor as a nation and as the people of God) is the subject that 'opens' the reading of the text and reveals the 'beyond' of the text. (Althaus-Reid, 1993, p. 367)

One can learn interpretations from before but one is not bound by them. As the poor read the text for the first time, they find different emphases, based on their own experiences. The Holy

Spirit, understood to be a mediator, continues to help interpret today. Life and Scripture still speak to each other.

For Juan Luis Segundo,[3] suspicion was crucial; one should be suspicious of how we understand our own reality, what ideologies influence this reality, and how the Bible has been read before. It is crucial to ask questions of ourselves, our systems and the Bible. 'The originality of Segundo ... is the incorporation of political suspicion into the discourse of liberation theology in Latin America' (Althaus-Reid, 1993, p. 388). For both Croatto and Segundo, the world and the Bible are both valid sources for theology and valid sources for criticism. The text itself emerged in a particular economic, political and social context; we can be attentive to and critical of previous interpretations, as we analyse our own economic, political and social contexts.

The key, however, is that no understanding is fixed. Interpretations should keep changing and emerging from new realities. 'As Ricoeur stresses, the reading should remain "open", that is, ready to break established codes if necessary, in order to produce a new interpretation of reality, and thus a new action' (Althaus-Reid, 1993, p. 350). If the text and life speak to each other, interpretation will change as life changes. Liberation theology works from the perspective of the poor and that perspective contains multiple aspects that change over time. Multiple understandings can exist side by side.

For Althaus-Reid, it is important to remember that God continues to speak today. What the hermeneutical circle recognizes is that God's words are not limited to the written text. Reflecting on a community discussing the Gospel of John, Althaus-Reid noted:

> this community, whose historical experience is reflected in the gospel, was not a community which exalted the written word to the detriment of oral reflections on actions and the value of culture as the product of people's hands ... God went beyond the text. (Althaus-Reid, 1995, pp. 11–12)

The Gospels show us that people were in dialogue with Jesus, not just reading a text. Not only did communities dialogue with Jesus during his time on earth, communities continue to do so today. 'The written discourse is always transcended by the non-recorded action of a God who overflows our theological and structural limitations' (Althaus-Reid, 1995, p. 12). God is present in the world today, as God was present in Jesus; much of God's action is not written down but simply experienced, even that which occurred during Jesus' lifetime.

We have sometimes forgotten God's continuing presence, prioritizing the written word instead. The excluded, the marginalized, in contrast, prioritize the text of their lives and their intimate relationships with God.

> It is a savage hermeneutics centered on the anecdotes of marginalized people's lives, and sets itself against the traditional ecclesial interpretation of the facts of history and the Word of God amongst the people ... Orality takes over the colonial writing experience. (Althaus-Reid, 2003a, p. 221)

Rejecting the written word and its authority, the excluded interact directly with God and each other. The excluded share stories with each other to better know God and to survive together.

The excluded do not fixate on the wording of the text. 'From the perspective of biblical hermeneutics, there is a rejection of the Bible as a colonial text, manifested in their lack of interest in the Bible and their doubt about the relevance it has in their lives' (Althaus-Reid, 2003a, pp. 221–2). The Bible's precise written text is not authoritative. In this reading of God's word, their own lives are key. God speaks in everyday life.

> The text ... includes the experience of everyday life that is 'read' as a Bible – a 'text' where God speaks and acts and can be understood ... They relate their appropriation of the biblical text to a future of economic, emotional and physical survival. (Althaus-Reid, 2003a, p. 222)

The excluded translate the stories of the text and their lives in order to survive. The written text and its prior interpretations are fallible; we can fail to hear and see reality. Just as God spoke to Moses and others in the Bible, God speaks to the excluded today.

The authority of the text is also irrelevant. Communities have their own versions of biblical texts, orally transmitted. Many of the excluded are illiterate and even if literate do not have access to a physical text. Preserving the exact text is a Western colonial emphasis. Instead, we need to privilege the understanding of the excluded and their connection to God. 'All communal reading occurs against a horizon of being that is similar to the one that surrounded the Israelite pueblo in the Scriptures: a particular, concrete "being in the world"' (Althaus-Reid, 2003a, p. 201). The excluded read the text and the world together, side by side, because they see similarities between their own lives and the lives of those in the biblical text.

The theology that emerges from the hermeneutical circle then engages both the written and spoken text and the experience of the community. Importantly, interpretation is not decided by the church hierarchy but by the people on the ground. 'It allows full participation in the process of rereading the scrip-ture or considering theological issues, without hidden agendas from the churches, that is, without trying to organize people's reflection into preformed doctrinal statements and understand-ings' (Althaus-Reid, 1995, p. 15). The excluded are in charge of their interpretations and theologies. They do not have to or want to fit into a hierarchy. Further, people build interpreta-tion based on reality, not publicized falsehoods, as discussed in later chapters. New issues emerge for theology, reflecting the concerns of the poor and marginalized, not the wealthy, patriarchal, heterosexual hierarchy of the church.

The final step in the hermeneutical circle is action. 'The pop-ular exegeses ... are validated in practices for change towards a Christian vision of an alternative society' (Althaus-Reid, 1996c, p. 389). A community is to see, judge and act, and this combination creates liberation theologies.

The hermeneutic circle reaches its end when, through a communal reading, the referential function of the biblical text (primarily its poetic or creative dimension) opens that community to its social problems, and encourages it to take on projects that address these problems. (Althaus-Reid, 2003a, p. 203)

The reading and analyses in community enable the excluded to act. Action is the final step and then reflection begins again, as the circle becomes a spiral.

The Theologies of the Excluded

Althaus-Reid analysed what theologies of liberation would look like if they followed the hermeneutical circle with those most marginalized. In Latin America, many people are not simply marginalized by the dominant system but completely excluded from the system. Althaus-Reid argued that 'Theology ... needs to start *from* and *with* the lives of the excluded' (Althaus-Reid, 1998a, p. 254). It is critical to begin theology with the excluded. Whatever emerges is a theology of liberation and continues the spiral of reflection and action.

Althaus-Reid highlighted the interpretation of the excluded because they live outside normalized structures. Where those oppressed but still included in the system in some way may still support and participate in its frameworks, the excluded do not. 'The excluded, by their very nature, are in confrontation with hegemonic systems, and so are liberationists; but the excluded are the ones in the unique position to surpass the colonial trimmings of Christianity in a way that churches cannot do' (Althaus-Reid, 1998a, p. 255). The excluded are not looking to fit in to any hierarchy, rather they work outside hierarchies. Beginning theological reflection with the excluded shows us how entrenched we are in the system and how difficult it is for us to analyse the system. Althaus-Reid noted, 'The pueblo start to ask why the Bible has been interpreted for them in individualistic terms, terms that convey the message that Christianity is about a reign of heaven and not about the work of God amongst the poor' (Althaus-Reid, 2003a, p. 203). The poor and marginalized discover things in the text that are different from what the churches have taught. For example, they find God on their side in the stories and they realize what they have been told is only one perspective that benefits the powerful. That powerful reading has been individualistic and has ignored injustice.

The readings of the fracasados (the rejected ones) produce several different theologies and understandings of God, Jesus, Mary and others. For example:

> The apparent 'multitude' of Christs ... represents the different perspectives of the fracasados' interpretation of God in Christ ... San La Muerte, Santa Librada, San Ceomo and San Son, are the faces of the 'Savage God' reflected through post-colonial spiritual voices. This God reflects the life experience of the excluded, their need for survival, and most importantly, the urgency with which they feel the need to make God concrete in their daily lives, on their own terms. (Althaus-Reid, 2003a, p. 223–4)

The excluded understand God in diverse ways – as death, as on the side of the poor, as strength, and so forth – as we explore in Chapter 6. Christian theology ignores their perspectives. To find God, we need to follow the hermeneutical circle with the excluded where God lives.

Unfortunately, liberation theology failed to continue the hermeneutical circle, as later chapters explore. Clodovis Boff,[4] a Brazilian liberation theologian, for example, advocated using the hermeneutical circle, but also encouraged guidance. While he agreed that being self-critical and critical of systems was important, he saw a need to keep some framework around textual interpretation. This combination formed a tension in his work between the authority of the church and the freedom of community. Althaus-Reid argued that Boff 'is afraid of the multiplicity of the discourse' that could emerge from different interpretations, but it is precisely the point of the hermeneutical circle to open text and theology to new understandings (Althaus-Reid, 1993, p. 337). In contrast, Boff wanted readings to remain consistent. One of Althaus-Reid's main criticisms of liberation theology is that it failed to follow the hermeneutical circle, preferring consistency over complicated realities. 'Simply, there were no structurally implemented elements for the empowerment required to exercise responsibilities in the church and in the nation, or to have all the voices of the voiceless heard' (Althaus-Reid, 2007b, p. 126). The structure of the church did not change to prioritize the interpretations or theologies of the poor. Several liberationists also followed Boff's lead in narrowing the allowed interpretations, maintaining hierarchy over sharing power. Even in poor communities, certain priests or leaders became 'guides', ensuring consistent interpretations. This guidance and limitation, for Althaus-Reid, must change.

Althaus-Reid concluded that the liberationist method, adapted and expanded from Ricoeur, was crucial in three ways. It helped to craft '1) the identity of the Latin American people; 2) the search for what Ricoeur calls a "positive utopia"; and 3) the praxis of change in the continent' (Althaus-Reid, 1993, p. 339). It enabled Latin Americans to interpret Christianity themselves, paving the way for liberation theologies. It is crucial, according to Althaus-Reid, that liberation theologies return to hearing and prioritizing the understandings of the excluded. We need to see, judge and act with the excluded.

Suggested reading

Althaus-Reid, M., 1998a, 'The Hermeneutics of Transgression', in Schrijver, G. D., ed., *Liberation Theologies on Shifting Grounds: A Clash of Socio-Economic and Cultural Paradigms*, pp. 251–71, Leuven: Leuven University Press.

Althaus-Reid, M., 2003a, 'Bible of the Fracasados: Readings from the Excluded', in Oduyoye, M. A. and H. M. Vroom, eds, *One Gospel– Many Cultures: Case Studies and Reflections on Cross-Cultural Theology*, pp. 199–224, Amsterdam: World Alliance of Reformed Churches.

Notes

1 Base ecclesial communities, as the name suggests, were communities of poor people, usually Catholic, who met to discuss the Bible and life and enact change in their communities. This group reading was in stark contrast to attending an occasional mass, which until the second Vatican Council was performed in Latin, so rarely understood. These communities began to be formed through the 1960s and some remain active today.

2 Beatriz Melano Couch (1931–2004) was an Argentinian Methodist theologian who taught at ISEDET.

3 Juan Luis Segundo (1925–96) was a Uruguayan Jesuit priest and liberation theologian.

4 Clodovis Boff (1944–) is a Brazilian priest and former liberation theologian.

4

Critiques of Latin American Liberation Theology and Feminist Theology

While Marcella appreciated aspects of Latin American liberation theology (LALT) and feminist theologies, she was also critical that these theologies remained within a 'heterosexual' framework. LALT ignored women, post-colonialism and the sexualities of the poor. Feminist theologies, on the other hand, ignored women from a variety of communities, and issues of sexuality, post-colonialism and economic critiques. Althaus-Reid wanted to both critique and further liberation and feminist theologies. While both theologies have the potential for liberation, as they emerged and fit into particular frameworks, these theologies lost their radicalness and became accepted as contextual theologies, failing to transform theology itself.

Latin American Liberation Theology

One would think that the outworkings of the hermeneutical circle would include a range of creative and vibrant theologies, perhaps even conflictual at times. However, what liberation theologians tried to articulate was one systematic theology: God is X; Christ is Y; Sin is Z; salvation is A. It did not consider gods, christs, sins and salvations, never mind crucifixions and resurrections. Althaus-Reid noted that 'Theology of Liberation has been and still is a subversive theology, but not a transgressive one' (Althaus-Reid, 1998a, p. 265). Liberation theology wanted to subvert the dominant theology, replacing it with another theology focused on the poor rather than transgressing the notion of systematic theology itself.

Where liberation theology stated that it would emphasize praxis through the hermeneutical circle, 'the fact is that over time Latin American Liberation Theology also developed its own orthodoxy' (Althaus-Reid, 2009a, p. 1). The hermeneutical circle was stopped from producing new theologies, as one formal theology developed. 'The "issue-based" theology pre-selected and actively banned the issues that were relevant to the people although inconvenient for the churches' (Althaus-Reid, 2009a, p. 1). Liberationists found a theology from the margins that could challenge the centre, economically and politically. Rather than continuing to let the margins speak, they stopped the process. Liberation theology could not deal with diverse theologies. It still wanted to find one systematic truth from the poor's perspective. Liberationists then narrowed their concept of 'the poor'.

For Althaus-Reid, liberation theology worked within the same frame as traditional colonial theology. 'The nostalgia for the past in liberation theology is a colonial nostalgia in the sense that it is built around a centrally defined knower, negotiator, and authoritative pattern, which unfortunately do not recognize emergent discourses' (Althaus-Reid, 2005b, p. 30). Liberation theology adhered to the colonial notion of a centre of knowledge; it assumed there was one true theology to find and one type of community that could find this theology: the poor. When varied critiques began to emerge from women, indigenous groups and homosexuals, liberation theologians ignored them.

Liberation theology only rejected some of the church's outworkings rather than the Western framework at its base. Althaus-Reid argued that rather than keeping their radical stance, liberationists wanted the establishment to accept them. 'Their ultimate authority still lies in the central church structures of the West and in the academic centres of Europe and the United States' (Althaus-Reid, 2004b, p. 129). It was important to liberation theology to have the church approve and accept its theology. Liberation theology was given a place at the table, a small space, seen as 'contextual', while theology without any adjectives continued as is. Theology could consider liberation but theology itself could not be liberated from its Western constructs. For two decades, liberation theology was published and discussed in North American and European realms, becoming more systematized and less related to theology on the ground. Then, the market died out. Traditional theology was happy to give liberation theology a niche, if liberation theology moved further from the hermeneutical circle, further away from the people it claimed to represent.

Liberation theology worked within the Western framework of dualisms: good and bad; white and black; male and female, accepting these dualisms as normative. 'Liberation Theology has evicted ... non-dualistic patterns of thought; non-hierarchical structures of thought and alternatives to non-reproductive and repetitive male epistemology' (Althaus-Reid, 2004b, p. 75). Liberation theology could not see beyond dualism and hierarchy to alternatives. Althaus-Reid argued that liberation theology became a form of colonial mimicry rather than the radical theology it started as. Liberation theology tried to become part of the centre, to be 'inclusive', rather than centring the margins themselves.

In narrowing, it stagnated. Failing to take a post-colonial analysis, liberationists saw political and economic oppression but did not move to consider other forms of oppression. It failed to see that 'Christianity in Latin America has been a sexual enterprise; it de-legitimized public structures and interfered in the domestic spaces of affectionate exchanges' (Althaus-Reid, 2009b, p. 9). Christianity condemned and destroyed the other ways of loving and living of the indigenous. Liberation theology did not see how Christianity oppressed people sexually and in fact continued this oppression.

Althaus-Reid argued that liberation theology should reflect the people in all their diversity rather than reflect church ideology. 'Liberation theology confronted structures of hegemonic power without questioning which epistemology grounded such power' (Althaus-Reid, 2007a, p. 33). Liberation theology challenged some of the hierarchy without questioning what underlay and supported the hierarchy. Liberation theology held to a certain moral tradition, which it left unchallenged.

In contrast to liberation theology, post-colonial theologies aim to remove hegemony, enabling diversity, rejecting one 'norm'. As Althaus-Reid argued:

> Liberationists are happy to find in the Bible Christ as the liberator of the poor but not to accept the deconstruction of Christ the subject, who, in some forms of popular religiosity in Latin America, emerges as a woman, the child of a dying mother, a corpse who walks, or even multitudes instead of an individual. (Althaus-Reid, 2004b, p. 128)

Post-colonial Christians recognize diverse Christs. For liberationists, Christ could be a poor rural man with some indigenous heritage but not gay or female, and so forth. Only approved expressions that were similar to Jesus' own historical context made sense to liberation theology. Liberation theology failed to see varying theologies among the poor.

Althaus-Reid highlighted that the excluded focus on Jesus as death rather than as life. From this beginning, their theology expands beyond what liberation theology anticipated. The excluded's theology rejects systematic theology and 'challenges the "small voice" of Western theology in Liberation Theology as structurally part of Western Christianity' (Althaus-Reid, 2004b, p. 140). The excluded do not respect traditional hierarchies. Althaus-Reid wanted liberationists to do real theology with real people, whatever might emerge.

So how has liberation theology avoided this expansion into the diverse realities of the poor? Althaus-Reid argued that 'Liberationists had forgotten what else may be due to the reflection of a theology using serious doubt as a hermeneutical circle, in the pursuit of God in justice and solidarity' (Althaus-Reid, 2003d, p. 130). Liberation theology stopped doubting once it found its own answers, rather than continuing the spiral of action and reflection. 'There has not been a consistent effort to reflect theologically using the full circle of ideological suspicion. By keeping class, gender, sexuality and race marginal ... we have made them ineffective' (Althaus-Reid, 2003d, p. 130). Liberation theology focused on economics and politics, as central, assuming other issues could be addressed later. However, this sidelining was to the detriment of all oppressive systems.

In order to ensure that the liberation theology emerging from the poor fit the appropriate pattern, liberation theologians began to narrow the theologies emerging from the hermeneutical circle. Many of the poor communities meeting to discuss the Bible and life did not focus on biblical texts. Academic theologians started to create guidelines for interpretation. Community leaders could then guide discussion. While liberation theology initially argued that any person thinking about and acting on faith was a theologian, one particular type of theology was highlighted. This type of theology again narrowed biblical interpretation. From her analysis of liberation theology, Althaus-Reid concluded:

> None of the great names from the liberationist ranks has ever produced any nuanced, deep theology which could justify a claim that liberation theology has heard the voice of the voiceless when ideologies of gender and sexuality have been the cause of suffering and marginalization of our own people. (Althaus-Reid, 2007a, p. 36)

None of the early liberation theologians included gender and sexuality in their analyses. LALT recognized class and politics but not other systems of domination. She argued this situation has to change for liberation theology to be truly liberative. Many people think about God and act from their own experiences. Liberation theology needs to reflect these experiences.

Liberation theology opted for the poor *but* not for all poor, just the 'decent' poor. While liberation theology claimed inclusion, 'The liberation theology project was never concerned with inclusivity but only with including *some* of the nobodies of Church and theology, the poor' (Althaus-Reid, 2007a, p. 26). While liberation theology is positive in prioritizing the poor,

'In the kingdom of God, the nobodies have the prerogative, as Jesus himself is the historical option of a God who became human by becoming a marginal, vulnerable Jew in a country under an economic, cultural and religious foreign occupation' (Althaus-Reid, 2007a, p. 26). Jesus was a nobody; nobodies need to be prioritized. Unfortunately, liberation theology continued to exclude people outside the 'moral' system, even though Jesus himself was outside the moral system of his time. 'The poor who were included were conceived of as male, generally peasant, vaguely indigenous, Christian and hetero-sexual' (Althaus-Reid, 2007a, p. 27). Liberation theology criticized the exclusion of the poor from theology but it also excluded some, those most marginal.

Further, liberation theology recognized the poor exploited by the system but not people completely excluded from the system. Althaus-Reid noted that 'people under the bridges are not talking liberation anymore but transgression' (Althaus-Reid, 1998a, p. 259). The excluded focus on life outside of the system entirely. This shift occurred, according to Althaus-Reid, because it was impossible to translate between the language of liberation theology and the language of the excluded. For example, liberation theology never challenged faith or the religion of Christianity itself and failed to address many issues of power injustices. The excluded still set real life and spiritu-ality side by side, working completely outside the dominant structures.

In particular, Althaus-Reid highlighted the failure of liber-ation theology to recognize the diverse sexual realities of the poor.

> Our poor have little to do with church patterns of sacralized, patriarchal families: they seldom marry, or live in monogamy, but in patterns of solidarity, characterized by accepting and mutually helping each other in a kind of affective network of extensive family relationships. (Althaus-Reid, 2007a, p. 29)

The relationships of the poor differ from the church's defini-tion of moral relations. They form loving relationships outside the boundaries of marriage and biological family. Rather than understanding that colonial Christian theology also brought with it a European notion of sexuality and relationships that matched the capitalist process, liberation theology kept the sexual frame while trying to reject the capitalist frame. 'Liberation theology ... assumed a dual universe of rigid identities between poor men and poor women without introducing any "hermeneutical suspicion" ... The tragedy is that liberation theology has not taken seriously the rich traditions of the sexually different in Latin America' (Althaus-Reid, 2005b, p. 32). Women and people of varying sexualities could not challenge liberation theologies' status quo, even though their experiences were clearly different. Liberation theology wanted to reimagine a new classless society but, 'these ideal pictures did not envisage any substantial changes in the way we understand loving relationships in society' (Althaus-Reid, 2009a, p. 1). Understandings of sexual relationships are closely tied to particular economic and political systems; enabling alternatives in one would most likely lead to alternatives in another; however, liberation theology failed to see the connections.

Althaus-Reid clearly articulated this exclusion of issues of sex and gender with the example of the poor celebrating carnivals:

> If the shanty townspeople go in procession carrying a statue of the Virgin Mary and demanding jobs, they seem to become God's option for the poor. However, when the same shanty townspeople mount a carnival centred on a transvestite Christ accompanied by a Drag Queen Mary Magdalene kissing his wounds, singing songs of political criticism, they are not anymore God's option for the poor. (Althaus-Reid, 2000c, p. 25)

The poor did not distinguish between political and sexual protest; they blend realms. While poor people continued to work towards liberation, their expanded theologies were ignored. It is time to explore their theologies and allow these theologies to liberate us.

While liberationists did struggle against political and economic repression, many liberationists also accepted some of the framework the military dictatorships encouraged when it came to patriarchy and heterosexuality. For example, 'there was also little solidarity on the part of the militant churches, informed by Liberation Theology, with the people who lived in fear and suffered persecutions and violence due to their sexual and gender options' (Althaus-Reid, 2009b, p. 6). Althaus-Reid argued that the military dictatorships operated under a code of 'decency', as we discuss in Chapter 9. Liberation theology followed this patriarchal and heterosexual discourse. Not only did liberationists avoid gender and sexuality, they criticized people for addressing such issues. The theological issues excluded questioning heterosexuality and patriarchy. Liberation theology excluded those outside the narrow heterosexual framework.

The emerging sexual critiques came from activists and the marginalized, not scholars. 'It comes from the people, excluded from Church discourses … There is almost always an analysis of production, based on Marx, which makes them consider the links between consumerism, desire and production in the present global capitalist expansion' (Althaus-Reid, 2009a, pp. 2–3). People on the ground connect a critique of capitalism to a critique of narrow heterosexuality. These liberationists apply a post-colonial understanding. 'The use of post-colonial analysis in Liberation Theology reflects the need for the deeper understanding of the sexual identity and spirituality of Latin American people' (Althaus-Reid, 2009a, p. 3). On the ground, people see the need for a broader sense of liberation, including ways of loving. Will we listen?

Liberation theology excluded real people and their complicated lives. For example, women did much of the work in liberation theology; however, men received public credit. Just as liberation theology idealized the poor, it also idealized women as mothers and lovers of Mary. Feminists working in liberation theology are sidelined, given a niche, just as liberation theology was given a niche in Western theology. Women are not supposed to challenge LALT but to be complementary. Women can contribute to liberation theology but not liberate it from its patriarchal constraints. In contrast to liberation theology's liberating potential, Althaus-Reid noted: 'For a theology that claims to be a theology from the political, one must reflect on the fact that it was Eva Peron who gave women the right to vote in Argentina in full opposition to the church and Christian theology' (Althaus-Reid, 2004b, p. 79). The church has often been more repressive than the political realm. Women felt excluded by the church, though they in large part remained faithful to it, and to liberation theology too. Liberation theology needs to seriously consider its attachment to patriarchy and heterosexism. If a liberationist female is not a mother and exclusively a mother, she is excluded, unless she is a nun. Women, even in liberation theology, were limited. Instead, liberation theology needs to understand that a gender and sexual analysis is as key to deconstructing oppression as are class and politics. In reducing gender and sex issues to secondary status, Althaus-Reid argued that liberation theology fetishes people, replacing real people with ideas. LALT turned idealistic rather than reflecting reality.

In essence, according to Althaus-Reid, liberation theology became 'decent'. If liberation theology was truly concerned about action first and theology second, 'then the struggle must have taught Liberationists about a Latin American society built upon heavy patriarchal systems of submission and mastery; of violence in the domestic and public realms; of intolerance and authoritative regimes based upon heavy androcentric hierarchies' (Althaus-Reid, 2004b, p. 80). Liberation theology should have seen the damaging effects of patriarchy and heterosexuality; women were clear about them. However, liberation theology failed to see this violence and intolerance, adhering to theology more than radical action in terms of women and people of other sexualities.

> According to [Guillermo] Cook, discrimination against women on grounds of a prioritization of tasks in the liberationist churches obeyed a principle of military strategy, where responsibilities are normally distributed in order to minimize casualties and be ready to act on short notice: grace is distributed according to a logic of profit. (Althaus-Reid, 2007b, p. 126)

Liberation theology adopted the military mode of a strict hierarchy of issues to be addressed. Decent liberation theology was
born, ignoring further oppressive structures.

Althaus-Reid argued that liberation theology needs to see
– the first step in see–judge–act – the beginning of the hermeneutical circle. As stated at the beginning of *Indecent Theology*,
'My purpose in this book is not to demolish Liberation
Theology *al la Europea* (in a European academic fashion),
but to explore the contextual hermeneutical circle of suspicion
in depth by questioning the traditional liberationist context
of doing theology' (Althaus-Reid, 2000c, p. 5). Althaus-Reid
worked within LALT but emphasized the spiral of action and
reflection in all arenas. A systematic liberation theology should
not exist because the hermeneutical circle should always continue. There should never be *one* theology of liberation but a
continuing spiral of action and reflection.

In sum, Althaus-Reid emphasized three areas lacking in
liberation theology due to a failure to use the hermeneutical
circle:

1 Issues concerning a post-colonial reflection on indigenous
   sexual and economic cultures.
2 The early influence of the work of Enrique Dussel ... who
   homologized capitalist desire with gay desire.
3 Finally, the development of a type of feminist Liberation
   Theology which ... did not question the ideological formation of sexuality. (Althaus-Reid, 2009b, p. 8)

Liberation theology failed to include a post-colonial sexual
analysis, actively prioritized heterosexuality and failed to
effectively challenge patriarchy. Attention to post-colonialism,
queer theories and feminisms can help rejuvenate liberation
theologies, as further chapters explore.

Feminist Theology

Althaus-Reid argued that feminist theology has taken strides against patriarchy. However, both feminist and liberation theologies need to move beyond what have become 'ideals' rather than realities, to dig more deeply into oppressive constructs. It made sense, for Althaus-Reid, that feminist theologians began with inclusion. 'That feeling of being born as a permanent Other to God, was a decisive experience at the beginning of Feminist thinking and theology. The first feminist theological wave wanted inclusivity' (Althaus-Reid, 2005c, p. 266). Women wanted to be represented in the body of Christ. What the search for inclusion showed, however, was that

> a metaphysical reversal occurred in terms of the equality paradigm. It was not we, women, strangers to God and minor male divinities, who wanted to be admitted into the heavenly and ecclesiastical courts ... No. It was the discovery that it was ... God himself who was a stranger for women, black people, the poor and the sexual marginalized. (Althaus-Reid, 2005c, p. 267)

Many feminist theologians realized that women did not need to be included; the conception of God needed to be expanded. The Western construct of God was not the God of the marginalized. It was a God constructed and boxed in by Western men. This is true of much Christian theology. It does not reflect the actual experiences of women, trans and people with varying sexualities.

Feminist theology, like liberation theology, became accepted as a niche, not upending traditional theology but allowed to be taught alongside. In response, it stayed along its path of gender analysis. 'Our women have many bruises in their lives: the churches slap their faces, men push them around and the welfare system punches them in the nose' (Althaus-Reid, 1996a, p. 73). Women are harmed by religious, political and economic systems. Feminist theology needs to continue challenging, moving beyond gender alone to become 'A feminist

Theology which could articulate a meaningful praxis for the homeless women who were sleeping in the street this Winter' (Althaus-Reid, 1996a, p. 73). It needs to reconnect to the lives of real women, real people who have varying sexual relationships, varying economic experiences and varying political perspectives.

Althaus-Reid was particularly critical of the European form of Mariology promoted in Latin America and beyond. Mary, as constructed in the Christian tradition, is not a real woman. While liberation theologians critiqued some aspects of Christian theology, they have left Mary intact and unchallenged. Althaus-Reid critiqued the example of Ivone Gebara[1] and Maria Bingemer,[2] who argued in their 1989 book, *Mary, Mother of God, Mother of the Poor*, that Mary could help to liberate Latin American women. For Althaus-Reid, Mary has been used to oppress women in Latin America throughout its history. 'If Mary is a symbol for the Latin American women's liberation movement, how is it that in 300 years we have seen exactly the opposite?' (Althaus-Reid, 2000c, p. 44). She urged an unpacking of the harm caused by the European Mary and an analysis of the diverse Marys that have emerged across the Americas.

Where feminist theologies began critiquing gender roles, the lives of the marginalized show us that sexuality is a key component of patriarchy too. Althaus-Reid added in this sexual suspicion, emerging from the lives of the marginalized, arguing that patriarchy relies on heterosexuality. Feminist theologies need to focus on real women and their real lives. Althaus-Reid argues, 'Feminist Theology needs blackness (gender and race), needs Otherness (sexuality and class struggle)' (Althaus-Reid, 1996a, p. 73). We need to empower and encourage women in all their diversity. Women can form their own theologies, from their own experiences.

Althaus-Reid wanted feminist theologies to move beyond gender to sex. 'The gap between a Feminist Liberation Theology and an Indecent Theology is one of sexual honesty' (Althaus-Reid, 2000c, pp. 6–7). Arguing that women should be equal to men doesn't challenge the sex binary or heterosexuality at its core. Arguments need to go further. Heterosexuality with its focus on marriage between one man and one woman for life should not dominate. Analysing gender leaves constrictive sexual norms alone. Feminist studies in general has moved to talking about sex and sexuality; however, feminist theologians have not – they should. Traditional theology constantly talks about sex and sexuality but not positively. Lust and eros are denigrated; instead, they should be celebrated.

Hence, both in liberation theologies and feminist theologies there continue to be blind spots and, rather than stay within the safe spaces that these theologies created for themselves, Althaus-Reid argued that these theologies must transgress their own systematization. God, Jesus, Mary, salvation, sin and other concepts must be subjected to suspicion for these theologies to be truly liberative and feminist. In particular, theologies need to take a post-colonial analysis, as the next chapter explores.

Suggested reading

Althaus-Reid, M., 2004b, 'Bién Sonados? The Future of Mystical Connections in Liberation Theology', in *From Feminist Theology to Indecent Theology*, pp. 65–82, Ch. 4, London: SCM Press.

Althaus-Reid, M., 2005b, 'From Liberation Theology to Indecent Theology', in Petrella, I., ed., *Latin American Liberation Theology: The Next Generation*, pp. 20–38, New York: Orbis Books.

Althaus-Reid, M., 2005c, 'From the Goddess to Queer Theology: The State we are in now', *Feminist Theology*, 13, pp. 265–72.

Althaus-Reid, M., 2007a, 'Class, Sex and the Theologian: Reflections on the Liberationist Movement in Latin America', in Althaus-Reid, M., I. Petrella and L. C. Susin, eds, *Another Possible World*, pp. 23–38, London: SCM Press.

Notes

1 Ivone Gebara (1944–) is a Brazilian nun and feminist theologian.

2 Maria Clara Bingemer (1941–) is a Brazilian Catholic theologian and professor.

5

Post-colonialism and Indigeneity

Althaus-Reid argued that a post-colonial analysis was critical for liberation theologies. She wrote from her Argentinian context, highlighting the indigenous communities that spanned the continent prior to Columbus' invasion and continue to resist colonization and globalization today. Examples of resistance from these communities appear throughout her work, as she applied a post-colonial analysis to decode theology, economics and sexuality.

Post-colonial

For Althaus-Reid, liberation theology remained colonial and failed to enact a post-colonial critique, as noted in the previous chapter. In contrast to liberation theology, which accepted the concept of normativity, post-colonialism aims to deconstruct what colonialism assumed to be normal.

> By 'Postcolonial Theology' I refer to the criticisms of that way of theologizing imposed by the Western world as theology. The postcolonial theological project ... problematizes such categories as 'the poor' and 'indigenous theology' because it is distrustful of the continuation of the Western ontology as the theoretical subject of theology. (Althaus-Reid, 2004b, p. 125)

Post-colonialism questions the assumed superiority of Western knowledge, in fact, the assumed superiority of any one knowledge. Where liberation theology followed Western thinking and homogenized the poor and thus excluded some, post-colonial critiques question any homogenous categorization. People are diverse and a variety of oppressions and privileges intersect and each of these should be attended to.

Important to a post-colonial critique is to end the hegemony of Western thought. What the colonial powers assumed to be knowledge is not the only form. Nothing should be taken as given; everything should be subject to suspicion. For Althaus-Reid, the difference between post-colonial critiques and liberationist critiques is that liberationists still accept the framework of Western Christianity, including systematizing theology (Althaus-Reid, 2004b, p. 128). The terms Western and Christian need not go together, neither should there be a systematic theology. People experience God in diverse ways. Liberation theologians were happy to follow the hermeneutical circle when it supported what the theologians wanted to argue but it found systematization difficult to combine with reflection.

> Theology struggles to keep people in line – a problem found even in Liberation Theology. It is not always possible to develop a theological praxis from the poor while maintaining systematic theological integrity. This dilemma is, of course, part of the colonial inheritance of Liberation Theology, which in the end struggles with the idea of the authority of the believer (and the poor believer) and the *magisterium* of the church. (Althaus-Reid, 2011, p. 444)

Liberation theology had to choose between systematization and theologies of the poor. As more differences emerged, the hermeneutical circle ended. Liberation theologians stopped questioning their own theologies and stayed with the systematic theology they were producing.

Colonial Christianity invaded Latin America, bringing several assumptions including a Western notion of time as linear rather than cyclical and that Western knowledge was *the* form of knowledge (Althaus-Reid, 2000c, p. 13). For the indigenous, everything was upended, from their understanding of time as cyclical to the way they saw reality itself. The Western colonial framework prefers narrow definitions and dualisms: good and evil, black and white, and so on. As we will unpack later, white and male became characteristics of purity; anything outside that box was impure.

Althaus-Reid argued that economics and sex were closely connected in colonialism, particularly with the understanding of women as property to be exchanged. Women were needed for reproduction and varied domestic labours; homosexual relationships did not produce children and so were unapproved (Althaus-Reid, 2000c, p. 20). The importance of marriage was to continue the male lineage and women were needed to give birth to and raise the children. In Latin America, there was a particular term for such oppression of women: '*la mala vida*' (the bad life) (Althaus-Reid, 2000c, p. 21). Oppression of women was the norm; a woman existed for male desire and to reproduce.

Christian theology is a sexual theology, thought out through capitalist economics, though it does not often acknowledge these connections.

In the *Conquista* of Latin America there was a Sexual Theology which ... [contained] the following points:

1 Deprivation of economic support and basic infrastructure of the home (the site of the female).
2 Legal physical punishment as the duty of a male to teach a female. The native as a minor.
3 Regulation of sexual practices inside and outside marriage. (Althaus-Reid, 2000c, p. 21)

A woman's world was at home; the public realm was for men; economics then focused on the world outside the home, the world of men. Women were considered inferior, subsumed under men. Indigenous people were considered children, inferior to the colonial men and women. Colonizers could own and use the land, its resources, women and the indigenous. The advance of capitalist economics accentuated this dominance and submission.

Colonial theology never searched for experiences of God among the indigenous; colonists assumed there were none. The construct of sexuality has benefited from post-colonial analysis in particular, subjecting colonial notions of heterosexuality and patriarchy to suspicion. While liberationists could clearly see the need for political and economic alternatives, they did not recognize the hegemony of heterosexuality that came with colonization. The church constrained and repressed indigenous ways of relating sexually.

Sin, Salvation and Colonialism

Colonial Christians assumed the Western form of Christianity with all its cultural assumptions was the only correct form and forced this form on to the indigenous, ignoring indigenous spiritualities and knowledge. 'The Grand Narratives, or the authoritative discourses which sustain everyday life ... collapsed in Latin America over the course of a few years ... "Tongues" were lost; mother tongues were buried while human tongues were cut from mouths' (Althaus-Reid, 2000c, p. 11). Colonizers destroyed people and their ways of life, deeming those ways evil and mandating European ways of life, including Christianity. For Althaus-Reid, salvation was exchanged for submission: economic, sexual and religious. Latin Americans are descendants of literal and epistemological rape, rape supported by the Christian church (Althaus-Reid, 2000c, p. 173). The church told indigenous Americans they were in debt to God because their way of life was wrong. Althaus-Reid told the story of Cacique Nicaragua, who was converted to Christianity by the colonizers. 'Why was the Cacique converted? ... Redemption and grace came to him as repentance of his mother tongue, his culture and his faithfulness to religious and political systems tried and tested by the collective history of his nation' (Althaus-Reid, 2000a, p. 68). The Cacique could only receive grace by giving up all his previous knowledge and culture. In fact, salvation was not free but cost the indigenous their ways of living, loving and knowing.

The Europeans understood the indigenous to need salvation from their sinful state. 'In the market of souls that the colonies were, not only were the goods of salvation dispensed but their need was created too' (Althaus-Reid, 1998c, p. 5). The church taught the indigenous two things: first, the indigenous needed salvation; second, only the colonizer's form of religion could provide this salvation. The indigenous were suddenly in debt to God. This economic understanding became a way of the world. The indigenous had to change their entire way of living and loving to attempt to get themselves out of the debt of sinfulness.

Traditionally, Christian theology argues we are in debt to God. However, this understanding conflicts with the concept of God's love for humanity, according to Althaus-Reid. 'Grace is a doctrine built upon a dualistic oppositional model. The opposition between God's power and benevolence and people's disgraceful state is exacerbated' (Althaus-Reid, 2000a, p. 66). Our understanding of salvation is based on dualism: God is great, humans are terrible. In the case of Latin America, 'The native is the subject of grace *par excellence* because in the construction of the native's fallenness (Paganism for instance) Otherness is epitomized and redeemed' (Althaus-Reid, 2000a, pp. 66–7). The indigenous were considered the most sinful of human beings. Because the indigenous were completely without inherent goodness, they could only rely on God's grace. 'They are "incorporated" to the world family of Christianity but they do not own theology, they just rent it' (Althaus-Reid, 2000a, p. 67). Their lack of goodness meant they could only receive theology, not craft it. The indigenous 'became the sacrificial goat, the carrier of the imagined obscure perversions of humanity' (Althaus-Reid, 2000a, p. 68). The colonizers gave the indigenous all the opposite (negative) labels to those labels the colonizers reserved for themselves.

Indigenous people had no say in what salvation and sin meant, and indeed today many of us cannot contribute to these categorizations. 'Doctrines are not democratically accountable, nor are many churches required to abide by democratic procedures, but this must change or church and theology will not depart from a colonial mode' (Althaus-Reid, 2000a, p. 68). Churches and theology are hierarchical rather than democratic. The hierarchy must be broken; the notion of only one path (economic, religious, sexual, etc.) must be broken in order for humans to see God and to build relationships with each other and with God.

A post-colonial analysis addresses the initial rejection of indigenous goodness. Traditional theology 'has kept Christianity alive, but as if in the law of the market: eternal life for the early deaths of malnourishment' (Althaus-Reid, 2000a, p. 67). Christianity lived; people and cultures died. With colonialism came salvation, oppression and death. In some cases, the indigenous surrendered to this perspective or were destroyed, yet alternatives continue to exist in many indigenous communities.

Re-reading the Scriptures

Christianity, heterosexuality and capitalism supported each other, excluding alternatives. Biblical interpretation supported this coalition. As explored throughout Althaus-Reid's work and in various sections of this book, the biblical texts contain accounts of colonialism, heterosexuality and domination of others, supported by the God of the biblical texts (Althaus-Reid, 2000c, p. 94). Colonial Christianity assumed Western superiority; that superiority meant colonizing nations could, and should, control other uncivilized areas.

Althaus-Reid suggested we read particular scriptures from below, challenging the dominant narrative, for example, the story of Rahab in Joshua 2. 'In this narrative, it is the mono-God of heterosexuality who calls for an original female act of betraying, as part of the founding narrative of the Promised Land' (Althaus-Reid, 2007e, p. 137). God requires Rahab to deny herself and her community in order for the Israelites to achieve their goal of owning land. For Althaus-Reid, as in the story of Lot and the Sodomites, Genesis 19, 'It is the God of Joshua (the same God as the God of the Sodomites) who is inhospitable, who cannot live with the different' (Althaus-Reid, 2007e, p. 138). This God appears to require a denial of anything different, which traditional readings do not recognize or highlight. The oppressed see scriptures from a different perspective, enabling alternative interpretations. 'Only a postcolonial analysis, suspicious of the alliance between European ideologies and Christianity in relation to the construction of people's identities and relationships, can introduce liberationists to new levels of hermeneutical suspicion' (Althaus-Reid, 2007a, p. 30). We need to read texts with suspicion, not simply accepting the dominant reading. Reading from below helps us to see oppression, dominance and misuse of power.

Althaus-Reid called the excluded's interpretation of Christianity 'savage hermeneutics', as we explore in the following chapter. Unlike the priority of the written text and hierarchy of interpretation, the excluded are free in their understandings. As noted in the chapter on the hermeneutical circle, for the excluded the 'text' is oral, the stories support their experiences, finding new meanings. Similar to the original base ecclesial communities, there is a focus on the people's conversation and experience. However, where liberation theology formalized the original experiences into a 'theology', the excluded remain free from this academic straitjacket. One major difference is that the biblical text itself is unimportant, as many are illiterate or do not have access to the text. Instead, it is the stories themselves as passed on through the community that matter, along with the experiences the communities have daily. What matters is a daily connection with God. Life is the text. The excluded connect to and speak with God through life and Bible stories.

Althaus-Reid argued that liberation theology needs to welcome theologies in all their diversities, even when they challenge liberation theology itself. Rather than accept previously articulated theological concepts, the role of the hermeneutical circle and liberation theology is to constantly reflect and act. The circle should continue.

Indigenous Perspectives

Althaus-Reid asked how colonialism still impacts theology. She framed this question in the context of the indigenous as the Canaanites, who are still destroyed in the reading of the biblical text today.

> We already know that the event of the destruction of Canaan is a performative act in colonial Christianity ... However, Canaan as a term represents a dynamic of loss, mourning, and the force of theological re-inscription. Is it possible to recover: 1) memory; 2) sense of others; and 3) belonging to a community (Valdes 1998)? (Althaus-Reid, 2006c, p. 40)

Christianity has not challenged the oppression of the Canaanites. However, it could, enabling the resurrection of an oppressed group. Can Latin Americans connect to their own history and culture, recovering their own identities? Can the indigenous resurrect? And can Christianity cope with this resurrection?

Liberation theology should take on board post-colonial critiques, even in the face of reducing numbers of Christians and Christian churches, to enable us to see God. 'Indigenous leaders from Central America have criticized the churches on the grounds that for over 500 years, they have been unable to incorporate any substantial, alternative, post-colonial changes into their structures' (Althaus-Reid, 1998a, p. 263). The churches stay in a colonial hierarchical mode. In contrast, listening to those excluded shows how they experience God; this experience crafts theology, whether it agrees with previous theological concepts or not. This practice would enable the indigenous to remember and continue their own traditions, which may or may not involve aspects of Christianity. In repressing the indigenous expressions of economics and love, Christianity repressed its own ability to understand God.

Aspects of indigenous traditions that continue to survive are alternatives to the dominant colonial Christian narrative. One such aspect is a more flexible and cyclical epistemology, as the indigenous concept of time was cyclical. For example, the indigenous understood the sun to be born each morning as it rises, die as it sets, and then be reborn the next day. There is also a sense of diversity; for example, the Aztecs included the identities of the groups they conquered in their variations, rather than forcing the conquered to assimilate. Many indigenous assumed the colonists would do the same. However, the colonists and Western Christianity chose duality and domination over expansion and celebrating diversity.

There are stark examples of the destruction of indigenous concepts, particularly with regard to women. Althaus-Reid noted the story of WOMAN, an indigenous deity, female, represented by a serpent. She was a warrior and a mother to orphans (Althaus-Reid, 2004b, p. 34). A story is told of the WOMAN crying in the night, ten years before the colonizers arrived, waking up the indigenous, who heard her wondering where she would take her people to hide them. And in fact, women struggled against the colonizers but the colonizers raped and killed these women. Female survivors tried to make themselves unattractive to the men, covering themselves with mud. Some indigenous women today still cover their faces in the presence of non-indigenous men, to avoid rape, and WOMAN is still excluded from Christianity.

Althaus-Reid offered several indigenous alternatives still existing today. For example, one alternative from Peru, called *ayni*, could help us rethink our relationship with God in terms of salvation and redemption.

> The traditional relations of economic and affective reciprocity amongst indigenous cultures in Peru have demonstrated strength ... the Ayni or 'tenderness' (Fioravanti, 1973) ... In a way, the Quechua people have an authentic theology of Land in which God's grace is manifested in the harvest but also in the midst of the community work ... This is not a system which is based on debt but, as the name says, love. (Althaus-Reid, 2007d, pp. 295–6)

In this setting, communities work together rather than competitively, seeing love as central to relationships. Understanding

God's grace as reciprocal and freely given would change our relationship with God and with each other, focusing on celebration and reciprocity rather than debt and submission.

Communities in Argentina and Chile provide another example of alternative relationships, with their rejection of land ownership.

> The Mapuches of Argentina and Chile refuse to sell land or sign contracts for land related property ... Taking this point into theology, we may say that Mapuches do not require a mechanism to enter into a covenant; the covenant is life already, and provided that life is respected, there is no other requisite. Grace is, then, a right of life. (Althaus-Reid, 2000a, p. 66)

These communities see land as shared rather than owned; it enables communities to live. We are already in relation with the land and God; it need not be formalized. We can form relationships with another, with others and with God without debt or formal exchange, in contrast to the traditional Christian interpretation of salvation and redemption.

Further, alternative ways of loving continue to exist. Althaus-Reid noted that some indigenous groups see marriage more of a rite of passage into adulthood than a permanent state between a man and a woman; the end of a relationship and the start of another is just another aspect of adulthood, not requiring any further ceremony (Althaus-Reid, 2003c, p. 116). Althaus-Reid urged us to reflect on these and other practices across Latin America, such as bisexuality, homosexuality and transgender experiences, to see new forms of loving. Althaus-Reid notes the approach to relationships by the Ramkokamekra-Canela people: 'Both women and men ... enjoyed open extramarital relationships ... It is interesting that married women not only had this right (or duty) to have extramarital relationships but they also initiated them ... Their attitude towards sex was taught from childhood' (Althaus-Reid, 2003c, p. 128). Sex was openly a part of the community and celebrated. Women and nature were honoured, not considered property to be exchanged. It is not that heterosexuality itself is wrong; it is that no one narrow expression of sexuality should be normative or condemned.

In celebrating alternative ways of living out the loving relationship between God, the earth and humans, we come to know God. There are still alternatives for us to find today.

> *Volver a nuestras almas* (to go back to our souls) is the expression Peruvian indigenous people use when they feel alienated living in the big cities of the white people and in need of a re-encounter with their true identities. They go back to the mountains, and they say 'I'm back in the mountains; I have come back to my soul.' (Althaus-Reid, 2004e, p. 34)

These indigenous communities feel disconnected from their souls when inhabiting the 'centre'. Post-colonial critiques of theology want the indigenous to find their own souls, to help us all to find our souls and connect to God.

The Excluded

Althaus-Reid highlighted the need to focus on excluded communities, which include indigenous peoples, but also others living in urban centres. The following chapter details these perspectives with an analysis of capitalism and the voices of the excluded. According to Althaus-Reid, the communities most able to question the system are those completely excluded by it. One such way that the excluded question traditional theologies is through their focus on death, a concept we explore later.

> The worship and the prayer to St Death is a rich example of a transgressor theology because:
> - It dismantles Actuality by deconstructing the falsifying of reality.
> - It understands the structural nature of oppression ...
> - It disorganizes colonial organizations such as the structures of the church. (Althaus-Reid, 1998a, p. 262)

A focus on death rather than life transgresses traditional theology by seeing reality and recognizing structural oppression, including Christian oppression. The excluded can see God without the blinkers of the current dominant system. The excluded's experience shows the irrelevance and harmfulness of much Christian theology and how it also, along with other systems, claimed certain perspectives as 'the reality', although false.

Rather than aim to keep things alive, theology included, Althaus-Reid argued that the excluded simply want to have a relationship with God and to survive. Churches in Latin America and beyond want to sustain themselves, want to sustain Christianity. The goal should not be growing the number of Christians but to see God, to experience God. A post-colonial analysis helps us achieve this goal, enabling the indigenous and the excluded to craft their own theologies and expand the understanding of God.

Suggested reading

Althaus-Reid, M., 2000a, 'Grace and the Other: A Postcolonial Reflection on Ideology and Doctrinal Systems', in Wolde, E. J. V., ed., *The Bright Side of Life*, pp. 63–9, London: SCM Press.

Althaus-Reid, M., 2000c, 'The Collapse of the Grand Narratives of Latin America: Theology and Sexual Mutilations, and On Liberation Theology: A History of Usury', in *Indecent Theology: Theological Perversions in Sex, Gender and Politics*, sections from Ch. 1, pp. 11–21, New York: Routledge.

Althaus-Reid, M., 2004b, 'Gustavo Gutiérrez Goes to Disneyland: Theme Park Theologies and the Diaspora of the Discourse of the Popular Theologian in Liberation Theology', in *From Feminist Theology to Indecent Theology*, Ch. 9, pp. 124–42, London: SCM Press.

Althaus-Reid, M., 2007e, 'Searching for a Queer Sophia-Wisdom: The Post-Colonial Rahab', in Isherwood, L., ed., *Patriarchs, Prophets and Other Villains*, pp. 128–40, London: Equinox Publishing.

6

Capitalism and the Excluded

Althaus-Reid critiqued colonialism, which works from a heterosexual and capitalist framework. This capitalist frame continues to oppress Latin Americans today. Throughout her work, she began with examples from those people excluded from the market entirely, not simply those exploited by the market. By examining the lives of the excluded, she criticized the capitalist system for its dominance and exclusion of alternatives.

Capitalism

Althaus-Reid first criticized capitalism for prioritizing money, profit and growth over human beings. When she was young, her family was evicted because of unpaid rent. Ignoring human beings, the system continued. 'In times of hyperinflation and liberal economic experiments, my mother and myself ceased to be people. Economic theories became people, and evicted us because somehow we became things that did not fit their scheme' (Althaus-Reid, 2004b, p. 74). Althaus-Reid and her family were excluded because they could not participate in the market. The system evicted human beings, preferring money, corporations and growth. The capitalist system cares nothing for people, only that money is continuously generated.

This care about growth and profit means that capitalism sees as positive any harmful impacts on human beings, if these impacts grow the economy. Althaus-Reid noted that when people need more alcohol or mental health medication because of economic despair, that is good for capitalism. Anything that results in increased expenditure is a good: even mental health problems, a car accident or an environmental disaster. We have not set up the economy to prioritize the good of all humans; instead, people are evaluated in terms of their benefit to the economy. When people do not grow the economy, the economy excludes them. 'For Capitalism, poverty, unemployment and exclusion are consistent with the polarization of the system' (Althaus-Reid, 2003c, p. 148). The economy simply focuses on growing itself through profit. People will be unemployed and poor; this harm is natural in this system. Under capitalism, the market is supposed to be the centre of life, replacing whatever may have been there before in terms of relationships. According to Althaus-Reid, rather than seeing capitalism as one possible economic system, we see it as the only and correct option underlying and directing all of life. Yet, economies could focus on people instead.

Capitalism depends on other hierarchies to enforce its dominance, in particular patriarchy and heterosexuality. To a certain extent, according to Althaus-Reid, Maria Mies[1] has highlighted the connection to patriarchy. Capitalism is based on the hierarchy of men over women (Althaus-Reid, 2000c, pp. 171–2). Class alone is not the problem; so too is the gender and sex distinction, which regards men as superior to women and gives men first place economically, ignoring traditional women's work, excluding it from the economy. While capitalism oppresses people regardless of sex or gender, it is most harmful for women and non-heterosexuals. Women have to submit to patriarchal norms in religion, economics and politics. Non-heterosexuals have to submit to heterosexual norms in religion, economics and politics.

Theology, the Market and Redemption

Traditional theology, at best, has ignored its implicit support of capitalism and at worst has actively promoted capitalism. Our relationship with the divine should occur outside the capitalist system. Instead, the church is caught up in marketplace ideology. The church markets and sells theology. Theologians have absorbed this perspective of capitalism, debt, profit and growth, understanding the success of Christianity in these terms as well. Theological concepts are explained in capitalist economic terms. Althaus-Reid argued, 'Churches are vast enterprises where capital is accumulated and invested for profit' (Althaus-Reid, 2004b, p. 133). Churches adhere to a capitalist business model, even in concepts like salvation. That capital, systematic theology, is accumulated through the debt of the people. No matter how much human beings work, the church argues, people can never erase the debt they owe God. Church and theology can help mediate this debt. The church uses theology to grow its congregations. Our souls then are traded in a marketplace of theology. If liberation theology is concerned with economics, it should also be concerned with how salvation and other theological issues are understood. If liberation theology critiques capitalism, it should also critique capitalist theological concepts.

Not only are theological concepts influenced by the capitalist system but theologians also work within the capitalist system. As labourers, theologians produce theology and consumers 'buy' or do not buy the theology (Althaus-Reid, 2004b, p. 107). People have to consume the theology produced or the theology is not deemed worthwhile in the marketplace. Churches ensure that people need church and theology, in order to make them marketable. If theology does not attract followers, it is a failure.

In economic terms, human beings need God to save us from our debt of sin. The church determines that price is through its theology. Traditional theology tends to argue that humans must give everything, submit completely to God. God requires our total obedience and repentance to erase the debt of sin. 'If the doctrine of grace ... operate[s] as a bartering system of eternal life for material exploitation, then we only need to negotiate grace ... The whole vocabulary ... is written using a highly commercial vocabulary: the divine covenant or contract' (Althaus-Reid, 2000a, p. 65). When redemption is considered an economic concept, we are simply trying to negotiate what amount of life we can have now versus what life we have after death. While some will argue that God freely gives salvation to erase the unpayable debt, the understanding of salvation is still presented in terms of debt and redemption.

This understanding exposes a paradox in the concept of salvation. On the one hand, God freely gives grace; on the other hand, humans are indebted, so much so that they cannot get out of it, though theology enacts plenty of rules to attempt to do so. Rather than think of ourselves in mutual relationship with each other and God, we base relationships on hierarchical exchange where one gives and another must give back to achieve some semblance of equality. Thus, we and God do not relate to each other because we want to but because we have to.

The problem with this understanding, Althaus-Reid argued, is that 'In Christianity it means the relationship between a creator God as a producer of life as a supreme good and a humanity subjected to a violent *ontological* external debt' (Althaus-Reid, 2007d, pp. 292–3). For traditional Christianity, humanity is in debt to God, a debt that, according to some theology, could only be paid through Jesus' death. For Althaus-Reid, because Christian theology has sacralized debt, this sacralization spills into other areas of life. We think about relationships in terms of what we owe or are owed. Humans are always in debt to God, or under threat of accumulating more debt, even when God has granted salvation. We cannot erase our debt or our potential future debt.

For Althaus-Reid, the precise problem with this formulation is that it is economic. The problem is greater than its attachment to capitalism; it is its attachment to an economic frame. 'The problem is not what economic order is present in the thinking of redemption, but that an economic order has become the hidden narrative and "Grand metaphor" of our relation with God' (Althaus-Reid, 2007d, p. 293). Our relationship with God is not economic. Further, focusing on economic relations means other violent inequalities are not addressed, as discussed in later chapters. In this economic understanding, human beings must obey God in particular ways. This conceptualization mirrors the capitalist system. Because capitalism and Christian theology reinforce similar concepts, thinking outside the box is difficult. The dominant systems support each other.

Theology Outside Capitalism

To overturn capitalism and other isms that oppress many, we need to rethink how we relate to God. Could we be in a mutual relationship with God rather than a subservient relationship? Couldn't we be in relationship simply because we love each other? Althaus-Reid stated, 'How we get free from debt by God's forgiveness or mutual forgiveness (as in the Jesus prayer) is not the issue, but why we assume that debts can and should be contracted' (Althaus-Reid, 2007d, p. 298). Rather than focus on redemption, we should ask why we see salvation as an economic concept. God is not limited to economic constructs.

Althaus-Reid argued that theology needs to understand itself outside of capitalist relations. She focused on alternatives that emerge among the 'indecent' and 'queer' people excluded from the system. Here, we can find ways to connect with God outside of the dominant system. For Althaus-Reid, we need to liberate God from these dominating economic constraints. She argued that we need to rethink God, Christ, Mary and other concepts. For example, we need 'to consider if our current Christologies (including some Liberationist approaches) should depart from cultural and economic metaphors which cannot challenge the economic structures of sin in our world' (Althaus-Reid, 2007d, pp. 299–300). Salvation and redemption have been explained from a particular economic perspective, emerging from a particular culture. What would perspectives from alternative economic and cultural systems show us about our relationship with God?

As noted in the previous chapter, we can examine how people interact with each other in alternative economic systems. For example, the concept of ayni in Peru:

> Reciprocity in community is understood as a part of a process of spiritual development. Feelings and emotions such as love or tenderness are considered important to manifest the soul of a person ... The economic goal of the Ayni is to minimize economic inequalities in the community by graceful giving, while improving people's living conditions. (Althaus-Reid, 2007d, pp. 295–7)

In this economy, community and loving reciprocity are key to a good spiritual and material life together. Alternative understandings continue to exist.

The Excluded

Liberation theologies need to move through the steps of the hermeneutical circle in community with the excluded to see how they live and think outside the dominant economic system. Rather than opt for the amorphous poor, we should opt for the excluded. Society has rejected the excluded completely. 'On Latin American streets, the Spanish word fracasado ... is especially reserved for the rejected ... Jesus was a fracasado ... [and] Scripture dedicates more space to the stories of anonymous fracasados than it does to such heroic biblical figures' (Althaus-Reid, 2003a, p. 204). A *fracasado* is a person completely outside society, as Jesus and many other biblical figures were. Hence, our theology should begin with the excluded. There are hundreds of millions of excluded around the globe. Their lives can upend our theology, if we allow them to do so.

> Anyone who has sat in a militant church around a table, together with the poorest of our poor of our brothers and sisters, knows that the bad smell left in the room by those who never have a bath or access to clean clothes creates more opposition amongst the members of the parish than the idea of a politically involved theology. (Althaus-Reid, 2007b, p. 124)

Unfortunately, we prefer to avoid the dirty, the 'mad', the 'other'. Rather than 'include', we need to give way to the excluded, not force them to clean up or to behave 'normally' in order to enter our churches and communities.

Althaus-Reid articulated the importance of beginning our analysis with those excluded from the current systems, as the excluded most clearly see the system's problems, be it our religious, political or economic systems. She delineated levels of exclusion, using Eva Montes de Oca's framework of 'the rings of hell'.[2] 'In the last ring of hell there are transvestites, transgendered beggars, ex-convicts, mad people and people who live under the bridges or in the huge garbage dumps ... The level of alienation between the people and civil society is almost total' (Althaus-Reid, 2004b, p. 148). Althaus-Reid focused on those completely outside society, deemed abnormal, crazy, and so forth.

The excluded are very visible physically, although ignored. In one telling example, Althaus-Reid talked about a public transport system announcement in Buenos Aires: '"The next passenger train is not for passengers" ... The announcement refers to the Tren Blanco (white train) that the scavengers take to go to the city to do their humble work of refuse collection' (Althaus-Reid, 2006d, p. 116). The train is full of people, but they scavenge garbage, so the system does not consider them as people. In cities, if you simply look around as you walk or drive, you can see the excluded.

From the system's perspective, the excluded do not exist. While some critiques of capitalism focus on exploitation, there are people so disconnected they cannot even achieve exploitation. The excluded do not participate in the market:

> such as Carlos, for whom to be exploited would be a dubious but real privilege ... The point is that the excluded have an invisible existence because they do not occupy the legal spaces of the construction of the social system. For instance, Carlos is not called Carlos ...Your name can only be said by a card with your picture and an official signature on it ... Carlos is the name of a famous boxing champion whom he admires. (Althaus-Reid, 1998a, pp. 252–3)

The boy does not even have a name; he simply does not exist in society. These people do not formally exist: no birth certificate, no citizenship, nothing. Society does not care whether they live or die; they do not count.

The excluded experience life in ways different from those included by society. For example, the passage of time is marked differently. The excluded's lives are measured by events rather than a consistent march of time. 'The excluded masses are getting younger, in a counting of history slowed down by the lack of meaningful, transformative events' (Althaus-Reid, 1998a, p. 252). While people included by the system celebrate birthdays, graduations and other milestones, such events do not exist for the excluded. Rather, their timing may be punctuated by deaths and other traumatic events. Each present moment either helps survival or could end it. Looking to the past or the future is extraneous.

Death is a rare constant for the excluded; everything else is temporary. Where flexibility is key to the lives of the excluded, so too is the presence of death, close by at every turn. Death will occur; however, resurrection is possible.

The excluded also form families differently from the 'norm', expanding and contracting them regularly, depending on their needs for survival and love.

> The most common form of family in the slums of Buenos Aires is called rejunte. The word in Spanish comes from junta, a gathering, and in slang re-junte means 'a new gathering' ... each time a new family combination is produced an old one may be recycled. (Althaus-Reid, 2004b, pp. 148–9)

Families are transient, coming and going, reconfiguring in the fight for survival. Families are also expansive, moving far beyond biological or marital constructs; they are made up of people who band together in the struggle for life.

Finally, sexuality in these excluded communities also differs from dominant normative constructs. 'When middle class theologians accuse the poor of being promiscuous they fail to see the presence of God in the solidarity of extended families

... the poor build communities around love and compassion rather than by legal ties' (Althaus-Reid, 2007b, p. 130). Poor communities expand the notion of family and loving relationships. Even among heterosexuals the idea of a marriage between one man and one woman for life is not the goal. The communities of the excluded form loving relationships in diverse ways. For example, in Buenos Aires,

> Transvestites tend to live in community in order to receive more support and protection ... For this ... is what a family needs to be, a place of nurturing of people and sharing experiences of life ... From the life of the excluded and their affective, family ways, Christian theology has much to learn – but in order to change and not simply to adapt. (Althaus-Reid, 2004b, pp. 164–5)

Marginalized people come together in community for support. Their families are not limited by biology or marriage. The job of Christian theology is not to impose a moral system but to understand how Christians form and live out their morals. How do the excluded love?

Christianity as it exists in the public realm of churches and formal theology is irrelevant for the excluded. God is part of their lives directly and daily, not mediated through the formal structures that exclude them. The Bible also exists in many forms for the excluded. The physical Bible itself can be protective and sacred. Some communities write out Psalm 23 on paper and add it to their tea (Althaus-Reid, 2003a, p. 210). The Bible enables the excluded to survive, beyond its words. Their theology is spiritual and material. God is physically and spiritually present. Further, many of the excluded cannot access the text or are illiterate. The Bible for them is a series of stories, orally transmitted from community to community. These stories adapt to changing situations over time; life becomes the text.

The excluded survive through a blending of spirit and matter. 'Logocentrism needs to be challenged ... Readings from the margins, from the fracasados of our society, can help us recover and establish the space in which biblical voices belong, that is, the space of the margins' (Althaus-Reid, 2003a, p. 209). Rather than focus on a text, we can see God today. We need to let the theology of the excluded emerge, from their current situations. God remains present today, not locked in the biblical text.

Their theology differs from predominant Christian theologies; dominant Christian theologies do not relate to the lives of the excluded. Instead, the excluded recycle, remake and renew theology to help them survive. The goal is not systematic theology, but a relationship with God that enables them to survive.

> Somehow the excluded elaborate a bricolage theology which corresponds to their own lives, a mixture of encounters ... with the aim of surviving. This is a very concrete form of theology which reflects experiences of nomadism, changes of family and geographical structures and a dyadic affective life which is reconstituted frequently. This is a theology whose aim seems to be a pedagogy of reciprocity and a reaffirmation of the courage of defying the centralized definition of love and success. (Althaus-Reid, 2004b, p. 152)

The theologies of the excluded emerge from daily life, reflecting their focus on the present and on their lives in community. The excluded reaffirm their own value and share a connection with God and each other, unseen by the dominant systems.

These interpretations move far beyond current tenets of liberation theology. The excluded pass on stories that help them survive. God and Jesus support them in their struggle to survive poverty, criticizing those who do not share the perspective of the communities of the excluded. The key is solidarity, not escape. The goal is to survive outside the system, not join it.

> According to the fracasados' view of life, the consequence of being a poor subversive is that one will refuse to accept poverty and, if necessary, muster the requisite courage to steal for the survival of one's family or community ... Santa

Librada is a female Christ who protects poor communities in which some resort to theft in order to survive. (Althaus-Reid, 2003a, p. 219)

Living outside the system also means ignoring the system's rules in order to survive. God supports the excluded in their rejection of the system. Their worship practices also emphasize a critique of greed and selfishness.

The excluded have many saints, some representing Jesus, Mary and other biblical figures like Samson. 'Divine figures such as *San La Muerte* (Saint Death), *San Son, Los Santos Bandidos* (Bandit Saints) ... exemplify the needs of different moments in the processes of exclusion ... Strength is sought and cherished through a recreated rejunte of biblical stories' (Althaus-Reid, 2004b, pp. 156–7). Again, these saints differ from traditional Catholic saints. Each saint responds to the needs of the excluded, whether it be for strength, protection or when facing death.

Althaus-Reid repeatedly referred to St Death, in terms of theological understandings of Christ. The origins of this worship are said to come from the indigenous, now practised widely but secretly among the excluded, so that it cannot be taken over or misused by dominant groups. As part of this worship, people have a bone representing St Death, slid under their skin, to make it a permanent part of their body (Althaus-Reid, 2004b, p. 159). St Death is a physical and spiritual presence in the lives of the excluded who cannot be removed by systemic forces. Death is a constant experience and expectation. Hence, the excluded emphasize Jesus' death rather than thinking of Jesus as life. 'Jesus Christ might be the Life of the World but for the excluded he is the Presence of Death, understanding death here as the equalizer, and the possibility of ending situations and starting new ones' (Althaus-Reid, 1998a, p. 264). Death is not the end but the place where all become equal, opening the possibility of resurrection.

The excluded recycle, resurrect and renew life, overcoming death by trying a variety of strategies to survive.

The art of el rebusque, literally to search and search again for little things that can help in the emotional recycling of the life and love of the poor. Rebusque as a concept shares with rejunte the 're' of repetition and as such it is usually found in popular expressions which indicate the sense of struggle among the excluded. (Althaus-Reid, 2004b, p. 162)

Rebusque, re-searching, enables the excluded to make it through another day. The lives of the excluded include a constant cycle of action and reflection as they attempt to survive.

These communities have developed myriad expressions of Jesus Christ, directly related to their lives. The excluded do not seek out the historical understanding of Jesus, rather they experience Jesus and God in their daily lives, tell these stories, and celebrate God in their communities, as God exists for them. The excluded find God in their own experiences. If theology cannot connect with these conditions of life, it is not connecting with God, because God lives and works with the excluded.

We are in the presence of an aesthetic theology gathered around the communion table of the excluded ... Without real bread to be found in the bins there is no transubstantiation. God's Eucharistic presence strangely depends on what can be found and sold in the streets. (Althaus-Reid, 2006d, pp. 108–9)

Finding something to eat in a skip is communion. Communion, salvation and survival is closely connected. Theology needs to reflect the lives of the excluded, reflecting real lives not imagined ideologies of capitalism.

Where capitalism and capitalist theology see exclusion as the norm, it should not be. Rather than trying to be included and exploited, the excluded work outside systems. It is here, outside the centre, that we can find alternatives to domination, in economics and in theology.

Suggested reading

Althaus-Reid, M., 1998c, 'Towards an Indecent Theology for Times of Development Impasse: Economic Erections, Global Erections', *Ministerial Formation*, 81, pp. 4–11.

Althaus-Reid, M., 2004b, '*Rejunte*: A Theology from Excluded Love', in *From Feminist Theology to Indecent Theology*, Ch. 10, pp. 147–57, London: SCM Press.

Althaus-Reid, M., 2006d, '"A Saint and a Church for Twenty Dollars": Sending Radical Orthodoxy to Ayacucho', in Ruether, R. R., M. Grau and M. Althaus-Reid (eds), *Interpreting the Postmodern: Responses to 'Radical Orthodoxy'*, pp. 107–18, New York: T&T Clark.

Notes

1 Maria Mies (1931–) is a German feminist sociologist.

2 Eva Montes de Oca was the author of *Guía Negra de Buenos Aires*, Buenos Aires: Temas de Hoy, 1995.

7

Women and Woman-God

In Althaus-Reid's early work, a key theme was the oppression of women. Women have been denigrated within Christian theology and within the capitalist system. She articulated the concept of woman-God through a variety of examples to show the alternative conceptions erased in the Judeo-Christian tradition. She urged us to consider God-woman to expand our understanding of God.

Western tradition has continuously ignored and denigrated women and women's experience. During colonization, colonizers raped and killed indigenous women. Even today, some women still cover their faces when near non-indigenous men to protect themselves. With the introduction of Christianity to Latin America, female deities were repressed; only the male God was allowed. This repression has continued throughout women's lives.

> Economic oppression is violent, poverty is violent. The mutilation of the God who is female into maleness is violent, and the exclusion of women from religious ministry, to which Latin American women are so accustomed in their original traditions, is very, very violent. (Althaus-Reid, 2004b, p. 24)

Christianity has caused harm to women throughout Latin American history. In particular, the Christian tradition rejected the woman-God. The biblical text was written by men, mainly for men, in a time when women were considered as property or lesser men, denigrating and excluding women. In addition, the one true God was understood as male, in opposition to any other gods.

Our economic, religious and political systems consider women inferior to men. In some cases, religion is more oppressive than other systems. In Catholicism, for example, women still cannot become priests and in some more conservative churches women still cannot take communion when menstruating (Althaus-Reid, 2004b, p. 100). We can reread theology from women's oppression. Until this point, men have defined the concept of 'woman' usually with characteristics that are opposite to maleness: 'the meaning of womanhood has been produced by the hegemonic ordering of patriarchal heterosexuality' (Althaus-Reid, 2000d, p. 33). Women need to define themselves, creating new understandings of themselves and God.

One example Althaus-Reid offered was how women are expected to interact with men in Latin America; women's eyes should always be lowered. If a woman meets a man's eyes directly, she is wanton. So too in theology, women's eyes remained lowered. 'Theology with women's eyes carried out exegesis, re-readings of the Bible, but never developed a serious feminist theological materialist analysis or hermeneutical circle' (Althaus-Reid, 2000c, p. 38). Women could append concepts to traditional male theology but not change it outright from their own experiences. The patriarchal categories of male over female remained. Liberation theology also discounted women's contributions. As male liberation theologians became predominant, they also made dominant a certain ideal liberationist woman. Once liberation theology constructed the ideal woman, it failed to consider this notion of 'woman' through the hermeneutical circle and it failed to allow women to craft and change theology.

For Althaus-Reid, theology itself needs to shift; much of it was crafted by men, for men. Hence, women have no language or path of their own; theology is always male-centred. One starting point is to think about women's sexuality. 'This I call the crucial point of "indecent exposures", that is, the beginning of a process of destabilization of theological representations of God and spiritual goods such as salvation' (Althaus-Reid, 2000b, p. 219). Women can expose the harms of theology.

Until normative theology is shaken, Christian theology has nothing to say about women, because it needs to reflect real women.

Theology from Women

For Althaus-Reid, God can be discovered through the experiences of women and the marginalized, a God who expands beyond the confines of the male.

> My search is for the deity in the female ... This is a God who disenfranchises Godself from the presence of colonial patronage in theology as well as being active in the Queer, alternative and dis-organized practices of social protest and transformation. (Althaus-Reid, 2007e, p. 131)

Where is woman-God? Althaus-Reid looked for her in women. God lives with women, resisting domination. Woman-God has been missing from the Christian tradition but is crucial for a deeper understanding of God.

For Althaus-Reid, women's experiences are the beginnings of indecent theology, as Chapter 9 explores. Rather than accept the repression of women, Althaus-Reid suggested the following: 'A more realistic, non-androcentric anthropology, ... indecent praxis of liberation for women' and the untangling of the theology around love and sexuality (Althaus-Reid, 2004b, pp. 88–9). We need to begin theology with real women's experiences, validating these experiences, and ending the suffering and harm caused by traditional theology, particularly around sex and sexuality.

Women need to write about who God is for them, not rely on male theology. This crafting is difficult as women have little of their own language. 'As women we must engage in the process of writing about who God is from our own experience, in ways that reflect our communities and struggles without any masks or dishonesty' (Althaus-Reid, 2000d, p. 32). We need to start from our own honest experiences. One does not have to use the dualistic forms presented by male theology. One does not have to counter male with female or father with mother.

Althaus-Reid argued that indecent theology emerges from the experience of marginalized women in particular. Women's experience shows us the failures of traditional theology to reflect either real women or real men. The suffering of women challenges theology as it stands. Women do not fit theology, yet they continue to exist and resist. Women's theology's 'strength is its prophetism, that is, the dynamism and analysis of the situations as they are in the present, denouncing the mistakes of the past and looking for a transformation which lies at the roots of the conflict' (Althaus-Reid, 1998b, p. 403). Latin American women are prophetic in denouncing injustice, refusing 'ostrich theology' and calling for acknowledgement of harm and death. 'The theology which encourages forgiveness without change has been called by Latin Americans "Ostrich Theology" because, like the ostrich (a popular animal in the continent), it puts its head under the ground instead of facing the situation' (Althaus-Reid, 1998b, 402–3). The churches and governments in Latin America have often failed to confront past and present wrongs, behaving like ostriches.

Women have been repeatedly told that their experiences are not sacred and that their behaviour is wrong. Althaus-Reid told the story of 13 Madres (women who protested against disappeared relatives during and after the Argentinian dictatorship), who in 1996 went to the Roman Catholic Cathedral of Buenos Aires to pray. The priest told the women to leave; when they did not, the priest called the police and the women were forced out of the cathedral, some injured in the process.

> Someone pointed out that the fruits of the Cathedral ... should be fruits of justice, of sharing in solidarity amongst the dispossessed and a project towards a society with peace and equality. Therefore, if the Cathedral cannot bear such fruits, it should be cut down. (Althaus-Reid, 1998b, p. 404)

The church needs to support justice; if it will not, it should be rejected. The church has repressed rather than supported women and continues to do so today; the church must change or die.

Women's experiences show us that we need to reconceptualize our understanding of commonly misused concepts, for example, reconciliation. 'Reconciliation ... has always been imposed over people ... as a way of not considering seriously the crimes that have been committed, the ideology behind them, and a transformation of the conditions which gave place to such violations' (Althaus-Reid, 1998b, p. 410). Reconciliation imposed by the dominant group does not fully consider what justice requires; it wants to forget the past rather than repair the damage.

The post-dictatorship governments wanted to forget the disappeared since their physical bodies were gone. However, these women remembered that we are all part of the body of Christ; ignoring one part does not remove it.

> Reconciliation [for the Madres] started then with an act of remembering as affirming the knowledge of the existence of a human being ... To stake a claim for the ones who are an important part of that body ... Re-membering is the Christ-act of final reconciliation of God with the world, in the sense of making God's people one body. (Althaus-Reid, 1998b, pp. 406–7)

Remembering is a form of resurrection, recreating the body of Christ and remembering Christ's death at the hands of dominant society. Each member of the body is crucial to the whole.

To be liberative, liberation theology needs to work from the experiences of real people like the Madres, not ideologies. 'The *Madres* acted by unmasking that false peace, and showing that real peace required political confrontation' (Althaus-Reid, 1998b, p. 405). Reconciliation requires forcing the perpetrators to remember what actually occurred and work towards justice. 'Reconciliation in struggle as shown by the *Madres* teaches us how the actual process of reconciling starts with a prophetic denunciation of the injustice amidst us' (Althaus-

Reid, 1998b, p. 407). Injustice must end before justice can begin. Support requires acknowledging injustice and struggling towards justice, not proceeding from a supposedly blank slate. This acknowledgement is important for governments and for the church.

Women have been in dialogue with Christ for centuries, crafting Christologies. However, traditional theologies ignore these Christologies. One aspect that was critical for Althaus-Reid in the context of Latin America is memory, as noted with the previous example. Recalling women's experiences throughout history is crucial. During and after the dictatorships, the 'reality' presented was skewed and not representative of what women actually experienced. 'What we want to know is what the women who struggle for human rights during the time of the *desaparecidos* can tell us about God, and God in our historical circumstances' (Althaus-Reid, 1998b, p. 398). Women's experiences and women's memories are crucial to understand God. 'The language of the silenced people, gossip, murmurs, denigrated by patriarchal systems as the fabric of lies and misinformation, is sometimes the only source of knowledge and communication when other forms ... are banned' (Althaus-Reid, 1998b, p. 409). Gossip has been criticized; however, it is how women pass on the stories of the real. Public sources are male-authored. Women's stories are transmitted orally and privately.

There is a rich vein of women's experience to form theology, although not often published. We need to examine historical and current experiences to allow theologies to emerge.

> Reconciliation is a word which literally means 'to bring together' ... Latin American women ... have added to reconciliation the further dimension of 'reconciliation in struggle', when their process of reconciliation is started by bringing together the people who stood against the dictatorship and reconciling them in an ecumenical, broadly based political alliance for the lives of the *desaparecidos*. (Althaus-Reid, 1998b, p. 400)

Latin American women have struggled to 'bring together' the reality of perpetrator and victim in order to work towards justice. We can recover these stories for theology, to better understand concepts like forgiveness and reconciliation.

WOMAN-God

Althaus-Reid reminded us that theology, and thus our concept of God, moves beyond the sacred text. She suggested reading texts from the Bible alongside other texts from life. One critical piece is to stop reading God as solely male. Althaus-Reid highlighted indigenous notions of WOMAN-God, which previously existed. As noted in the chapter on post-colonialism, women saw WOMAN as a model to follow, as a warrior. Images of the WOMAN had her wearing a skirt with stars and serpents, both representations of her. We can consider WOMAN and other conceptions of female divinity, and how society has denigrated them, for example references to serpents as negative in the Jewish and Christian traditions.

God-woman gives us important knowledge of God, linked to our lives, and reminds us how each of us represent God, even those of us society denigrates or excludes.

> God-woman reminds us of how material and bodily is the Christian conception of God ... Many people cannot imagine Jesus-Woman, washing her menstrual towels or going through all the indignities that women need to go through when they intelligently and courageously defy patriarchalism. Neither is it easy for many to envisage God-Woman as an old crone. (Althaus-Reid, 2000d, pp. 33–4)

We are all made in the image of God. We should be able to see God in every woman and in her actions, however mundane. Each of us represents a vision of God. We can only come to know God through seeing God in others, even those we might wish to avoid.

Further, God the female is not limited to God the mother.

We do not simply have to replace male terms with the female opposite. 'The language of "Mother Church" evokes a paternalistic model of an institution acting on our behalf, in which the "Mother" lives far away and writes international agreements without consultation: on redemption; on markets and on sexual arrangements' (Althaus-Reid, 2000d, p. 32). Mother, like father, tends to craft another hierarchy rather than a mutually dependent relationship. The mother provides rules, makes decision for us, and we are her children not her equals. We may want to consider different ways of relating to God, for example a partnership.

Althaus-Reid also explored the concept of God as a female prostitute. The idea came from walking through her neighbourhood with its many sex workers. There she saw Georges Batille's novel, *Madame Edwarda*, in a bookshop. In this novel, Madame Edwarda, a prostitute, is God.

> An anguished person searching for divine meaning in life encounters a prostitute in a brothel (Madame Edwarda) and she reveals herself as God. It is not through her words though, but in the intimacy of his relationship with Madame Edwarda and in the vision of her body ('Look … Kiss me!') that he receives the revelation of her transcendental, yet so bodily grounded divinity. (Althaus-Reid, 2000b, p. 207)

This God reveals Godself through bodily actions, not just words, and to just one person. Althaus-Reid notes that, surprisingly, systematic theology has ignored this text. Yet, it is finding God and Christ in the marginalized that helps us to better know God.

Althaus-Reid articulated three aspects to begin this reflection on a broader God, particularly from a female perspective. Where traditional notions of the Christian God ignored the feminine; the feminine as sacred cannot be ignored with God as a female prostitute, neither can sexuality. Next, God as a female prostitute shows the connections or lack thereof between women's poverty and God. The fact that we cannot see God in a sex worker shows us that we do not believe all to have the face of God. Yet God and Jesus exists in each of us. 'Third, it makes obvious that our problem is [that] ... our work is deeply attached to a theological method of discernment and representation embodied in the ideals of Androcentric Systematic Theology' (Althaus-Reid, 2000b, p. 208). When we cannot find God in a prostitute, it is partly because our God-language is male-focused. God the prostitute offers us a way to discuss God in female terms and outside of the 'ideal' woman.

Being able to see God in a prostitute would lead us to question both God and society as commonly accepted. 'Madame Edwarda as Woman-God carries the excess of many crosses: sexual abuse and poverty; misery and destitution; but also fierce independence and resolution of self-satisfaction. She is a God who knows and honours her desires' (Althaus-Reid, 2000b, p. 221). God can be abused, poor, strong and determined altogether. Liberation theology should begin with such realities of life, not expectations or ideals. These realities challenge our understandings of traditional theological concepts. Althaus-Reid articulated this as indecently exposing God. If our only image of God is a benevolent grandfather or father, we have not seen God in the least of these.

Women, Jesus and Mary

Feminist and liberation theologies also wanted decent ideal women; however, for Althaus-Reid, real women are indecent and this indecency is positive. 'Liberation Theology ... fails to confront the questions that women are asking about the male constructed Christ. The first question concerns the entirely God-male affair accentuated by the Israelite boy born to be God who Jesus has come to be' (Althaus-Reid, 2004b, pp. 85–6). For Althaus-Reid, indecent women can challenge theology at its core, understanding that even Jesus and God need to be challenged with regard to gender and sex-framed behaviour. The hermeneutical circle would shed light on the gap between the assumed 'ideal' woman and what women's experiences and desires actually were, if allowed to continue.

We need to begin with women's realities to see where theology ignored and harmed them with its male focus, stemming even from the male messiah.

For Althaus-Reid, women's experience can challenge Jesus, the male messiah. Jesus remained constrained by the culture of his time. In particular, Althaus-Reid cited the text from Mark 5.25–34 of the bleeding woman. Jesus heals the woman, rather than challenging society. Jesus continues these systems, enabling the woman to participate in them through healing. So, too, the woman did not ask society to change. The woman and Jesus accepted that female blood polluted. Women today can help to correct the androcentrism of Christ. Women can form a community with Christ, dialoguing rather than simply accepting the Jesus Christ presented throughout history.

> This Christ-Community is precisely an attempt to give meaning to Christ in a process where the community of women keeps completing it permanently, in the past, present and future. The genealogy of women such as the woman from Mark (who stakes a claim from her body, censured for its monthly production of blood), the women massacred during the invasion of the Americas during the sixteenth century, and the mothers of the disappeared in Argentina claiming the blood of their dead, give meaning to Christ. (Althaus-Reid, 2004b, p. 56)

Women's experiences, historical and current, are set alongside Christ's experiences in community. Together they form Christ, a Christ in dialogue, still becoming.

So, too, we need to challenge Mary and Mariology. Althaus-Reid argued that in Latin American culture Mary has been repressive rather than liberative. Just as all indigenous women were considered whores, so, too, educated women during the Argentinian dictatorship were deemed whores, told to go home and pray to Mary. Mary, as brought by the Europeans, is a 'rich white woman who does not walk' (Althaus-Reid, 2004b, p. 30). She does not speak to the needs of women in Latin America. Althaus-Reid argues that Latin American women should reject not only the patriarchal God but also the rich white Virgin. Mary has been used to defend rather than challenge dominant systems. Mary the submissive mother replaced woman-God.

Reading the story of Joseph, Mary and Jesus as a model for Latin American families to imitate becomes absurd for Althaus-Reid. She stated, 'I may start a Latin American reading on the mother of the family, Mary, as a dead girl, and Jesus as the son of a dead girl' (Althaus-Reid, 2000c, p. 99). For Althaus-Reid, seeing Mary as dead or inhuman helps us begin a different reading, shows us a different perspective on women. This concept changes the orientation of the family immediately. In fact, the Holy Family disappears women. First, the messiah is male, not female; no female Messiah is born. Second, Mary is not a full human being, since she gives birth without ever having sex. Even Joseph, the father, plays a minimal role. For Althaus-Reid, this combination means the story aborted real women. Women, as women, do not exist here.

One could argue the importance of Mary as Jesus' mother, since God apparently needed a human woman to give birth to Jesus. Instead, Mary seems to be a piece of property, as women were treated during that time. While it is Mary who gives birth to and raises Jesus, 'Mary ... disappears in the process of Christology by the appropriation of her unpaid Messianic reproductive work by the male religious community' (Althaus-Reid, 2004b, p. 88). Neither Mary nor Jesus are treated as fully human, and Mary fades from the story after giving birth. In fact, in the Catholic tradition, not only did Mary conceive while a virgin, she remained a virgin her entire life. We also learn nothing about her raising Jesus-child.

Mary's sexuality is denied. She did not experience all that a woman might experience; she is raised to sainthood without being a real woman. 'If it is true that the first inscriptions (of hunger, pain and sexual desire) are always written in the body, one wonders how a women's theology can start with Mary, the icon of a no-body' (Althaus-Reid, 2000c, p. 39). In this way, Latin Americans identify Mary more with goddesses than human women. Further, for Althaus-Reid, the idea that God would simply use a woman to produce a child is not surprising for Latin American women used to powerlessness and rape. Mutually respectful and enjoyable sex is difficult to discuss based on this text. Women cannot hope to imitate Mary, even if they want to.

Althaus-Reid explored alternative conceptions of Mary and Jesus that have emerged in Latin American culture. 'Another image of Jesus worshipped by the excluded in Buenos Aires is the female Christ, who stands crucified as a woman-Jesus and carries the name of Librada ... This She-Christ reverses the alienating male construction of divinity of European Christianity' (Althaus-Reid, 1998a, p. 264). Librada blends Mary and Jesus together, bringing an aspect of female to the divine. In transgressing the separation between Mary and Jesus, this worship also transgresses other areas of theology.

One other image of Mary is found in the Deceased Correa. The Deceased Correa represents a woman who escaped to the desert with her baby but died. The baby survived by continuing to breast feed. This is an indecent Mary, breasts out in the open, nurturing a child while dead. This Mary takes care of poor women, supporting them in whatever actions they need to take to survive.

> The Deceased Correa is an unstable and generous virgin who redistributes wealth and health amongst the poor, but also redistributes the grace of the poor women, the prostitutes, the *mujeres con pasado* (women with a sexual past), and sees the divine in the indecent acts of the everyday struggles of life for bread and for love. There is so much more to Mariology in Latin America than the Virgin of Guadalupe if we do theology with indecent intentions. (Althaus-Reid, 2000c, pp. 85–6)

The Deceased Correa protects women, whatever their behaviour and situation, and enables them to survive, walking with them in their daily lives. The Marys of the poor can change our theology, if we listen to them.

Where traditional theology has excluded and denigrated women and woman-God, it has limited our understanding of God. Instead, we can begin from women's experiences to find the sacred in each woman. Such examination will shift our theologies and concepts of God, Jesus, Mary, sin, salvation and so forth. This examination of our experiences begins with our bodies, as the next chapter explores.

Suggested reading

Althaus-Reid, M., 1998b, 'Reconciliation in the Struggle: Theological Reflections from the Rebellious Women of Latin America', in Butler, B., ed., *Open Hands: Reconciliation, Justice and Peace Work around the World*, pp. 397–411, Bury St Edmunds: Kevin Mayhew.

Althaus-Reid, M., 2000b, 'Indecent Exposures: Excessive Sex and the Crisis of Theological Representation', in Isherwood, L., ed., *The Good News of the Body: Sexual Theology and Feminism*, pp. 205–22, New York: New York University Press.

Althaus-Reid, M., 2004b, 'On Wearing Skirts Without Underwear: Poor Women Contesting Christ', in *From Feminist Theology to Indecent Theology*, Ch. 5, pp. 83–94, London: SCM Press.

8

The Whole Body

Throughout Althaus-Reid's work, a focus on the body is key. She clearly criticized both theology and economics for their ignoring, excluding and denigrating real bodies. She theologized from the body, in particular the excluded body.

Althaus-Reid noted the oddity of the fixation with controlling the body in Christianity, although its framework revolves around the dualism of body and soul, prioritizing the soul. Christianity is built on bodies, beginning with the incarnation through Jesus and includes his crucifixion (Althaus-Reid, 2000c, pp. 18–19). Christianity centres on God becoming human in Jesus, yet bodies are denigrated, women's bodies in particular. Althaus-Reid called traditional theology pornographic in its scripting of the behaviour of bodies (Althaus-Reid, 2004b, p. 99). Theology espouses posed acts of sex and other behaviours rather than reflecting reality; it then imposes this pornographic view on others, critiquing real lives.

The laws, rituals and theology passed down to us have mutilated the bodies of women and men, for example through circumcision, rituals around menstruation and childbirth, veiling and other bodily coverings. Theology condemns bodies as naturally given; bodies require purification to be worthy of God. Inferior to God, somehow human bodies need improvement, just as the spiritual selves do, even though humans are created in the image of God. Althaus-Reid argued: 'In fact, the crucifixion itself seems to act as the teleological divine act where the body needs to be ultimately cut and crushed in order for God to be Godself again' (Althaus-Reid, 2008b, p. 75). The human Jesus is killed and resurrected, recreating God but killing the body. Yet, that resurrected body is still a physical body, according to Scripture.

In sum, Althaus-Reid wanted us to recognize that only through our bodies in their diversity and experiences can this denigration be overcome. 'Coya women kneel in the church mixing the odour of their sexuality with their prayers, while their babies sleep on their backs wrapped in an apron ... And that is a starting point for a Christology done from women's bodies' (Althaus-Reid, 2004b, p. 83). Theology should begin with real bodies and real experiences. No part of our body should be excluded or condemned.

Incarnation

Considering God becoming human unsettles our notions of bodies as somehow less than the soul. 'Life can never be normal for those who embrace the flesh as divine, those who are lovers of God through that flesh in all its diverse glory. Theology that has incarnation at its heart is queer indeed' (Isherwood and Althaus-Reid, 2004, p. 7). God did not rescue humanity from being human; instead, God became human through Jesus. This changes our relationship to bodily loving God.

If we think about bodies and the bodily Jesus, as indecent and queer theologies do, theological concepts change. 'That God is in flesh changes everything, yet it has been a message of salvation in the hands of the Church which by its very nature does not like change – it is too destabilizing for its power base' (Isherwood and Althaus-Reid, 2004, p. 7). We can begin with the notion of God becoming human through Jesus; Christian theology has not fully considered the implications of the incarnation. God becoming human should expand and upend our theologies; yet this upending has not occurred within traditional theology.

God entered the world as a full human being, not as half-divine and only experiencing positive bodily functions, but fully human and divine. 'It is not the genetically modified, metaphysical Son of God that declares the divine-human conjunction, but the screaming baby born amidst the cow shit and fleas, covered in his birthing blood ... who declares salvation for all' (Isherwood and Althaus-Reid, 2004, p. 7). Mary, too, played a key role in raising this child, though this story is not told. God became a helpless baby, a toddler, a teenager, a young adult, and yet the stories told are only of the final few years of his life. God in Jesus lived through situations of poverty, homelessness and other oppressions, many of which we know nothing about.

> God has become in Jesus part of the order of sensuality by tact, by birth ... Jesus's birth is the condition of touching, or tenderness and sexuality not ordered as yet by law or custom because it displaces the idea of sexuality associated with productivity. (Althaus-Reid, 2004a, pp. 395–6)

Where Mary remains untouched, Jesus is fully immersed in the human senses. Jesus' body presents us with the divine/fully human combination. Hence, theology should not ignore or denigrate bodies.

Indecent and queer theologies take feminisms' focus on the body further, past gender and into sex. 'From a Queer theological perspective, incarnation acts as a classical fetishist act which does not accept the construed frontiers between the material and the spiritual but transgresses them both' (Althaus-Reid, 2008b, pp. 72–3). Indecent and queer theologies start with God becoming human in Jesus; rejecting the split between the spiritual and material or the prioritization of one over the other. These theologies also want to move beyond women's bodies alone, including the experiences of trans people. The call to examine our bodies does not mean we cannot wish to change our bodies but it matters why we do so.

Althaus-Reid gave as one example of our desecration of bodies the story of the body of a young boy, tortured and murdered.

> Monito Galvan, with his T-shirt inscribed with fashionable logos, was no Christ (the Logos) because crucifixion in

Bancalari has reverted to what it was in the Roman empire, a form of deadly torture. The simulacrum is in reality more factual than theologies, in the sense that his body showed the reality of death by torture, including the mockery of crowning him 'the king of glue sniffing', with the symbol of the plastic bag wrapped around his head. (Althaus-Reid, 2003c, p. 150)

This boy was tortured, killed and 'crowned'. What does seeing the dead body of a young boy do to our theologies? Can we reconnect to the real horror of the crucifixion? Have we lost our horror of torture and death? Have we lost our respect for bodies?

Real Bodies

Seeing real bodies and doing theology from these bodies should change our theology, which has tended to prioritize the spiritual over the material. 'Our hunger for food, hunger for the touch of other bodies, for love and for God; a multitude of hungers never satisfied which grow and expand ... like a carnival of the poor, the textbooks of the normalisers of life' (Althaus-Reid, 2000c, p. 200). Our bodily desires and our spiritual desires are God-given and lead us to God. Our desires are insatiable and God fulfils in God's expansiveness.

Bodies, including excluded bodies, are created in the image of God. Recognizing God in these bodies is crucial to building a more just world.

Social justice and a spirituality of the struggle have been constructed upon a ghostly race of rebellious corpses ... In liberation theology, the Other ... was given a face, a name, and a surname, together with a refusal to accept its own destiny ... the destiny to disappear from politics and theology alike. (Althaus-Reid, 2007c, p. 144)

The dead and excluded bodies are named and remembered in spite of the system's attempt to forget them. However, it is not enough to recognize and remember, we must also not formalize or normalize but allow diversity. Liberation theology began to focus on the body, an important first step. Unfortunately, it stopped at the poor, male, heterosexual body. However, bodies and bodily experiences are diverse and God is present in each body.

The realities of these excluded bodies should change our theologies because the experiences of the excluded are diverse, and remain outside our hierarchical systems, while most theology remains within these systems.

> It is only from the body of aliens in the history of theology (for instance, women, natives …) that hermeneutical avenues bring us new promises to old theological practices … They also form the unbeliever's body, that is, a body which has stopped believing in divine sexual grand narratives. (Althaus-Reid, 2003c, pp. 30–1)

Being an alien or a foreigner means bringing a new perspective; 'atheists' who reject the God of the centre form new theologies of the margins. There is no one theology, no one image of God. Instead, theologies and bodies are multiple parts of one body, the body of Christ.

The body is important in part because theology is material as well as spiritual. 'Queer theologies have a way of knowing/loving God that gives form to a different location of a theology of the spiritually concrete and the materially spiritual' (Althaus-Reid, 2007c, p. 137). Part of our materiality and spirituality is sexuality. We need to consider how our bodies are in relation to each other and to God, not how theology has constructed bodies. How do our spirits and our bodies live and love together?

Beginning with the body, especially parts of the body that have been denigrated, we can find new ways of knowing God. 'The point is that by queering body theology we may be led to discover the traces of a queer God, and through that the traces of Other covenants, lost pacts and revelations of God in an underground history of love' (Althaus-Reid, 2007c, p. 142). God exists in places we have condemned without searching; hence, we need to search these locations to know God.

Doing theology from women's bodies means we must first acknowledge the reality of our bodies and our experiences. Christianity does not help us discover the sacred in the female or in non-heterosexual experiences. Instead, we have to learn from our own stories. Much of what is pleasurable we have been taught to repress.

> From sexual story-telling studies we learn from the voices of women and men how the system in which we live is organized by making the unusual usual, that is, by enforcing gender construction considered normal by legislative means, in order to disrupt and tame the different manifestation of sexual behaviours in society. (Althaus-Reid, 2004b, p. 92)

The 'norm' is actually less common than the 'abnormal' and it is these abnormalities that can upend theology. Among women and the excluded, a whole variety of ways of being and knowing exists.

Althaus-Reid argued that it is not only the body that is ignored and constrained by theology but the body in love. 'We want to refer to the body in love, which has been notoriously absent in theology … This highlighting of the "ordinariness" of love and sexuality as done in a materialist theological framework belongs to the order of Others' (Althaus-Reid, 2003c, p. 113). Bodies and love are almost so mundane as to be excluded. Yet, they are key to theology. Love happens every day. We need to examine the diversity of the experiences of our bodies. Althaus-Reid focused on bodies in sexual relationships, to learn about loving.

Colonialism has limited understandings of love to a narrow heterosexual frame and so we need to decolonize love. 'If locating bodies in love in theology tends to follow colonial relationships, queering theology should always start by betraying love, displacing the construction of bodies in love, and creating opportunities to find God in unexpected places' (Althaus-Reid, 2007c, p. 148). Althaus-Reid suggested 'betraying' normative love from our own experiences. Latin Americans writing queerly do so from their experiences in varied realms, not just theology, not just having sex, but seeing it all connected. 'The interesting thing about Latin American queer writing is precisely the construction of bodies at the intersection of several discourses: political, heterosexual, cultural, and religious' (Althaus-Reid, 2007c, p. 149). We can unpack the intersections of oppressions to see new ways of loving ourselves, others and God, and where these have been denied.

As we look at our bodily experiences, Althaus-Reid urged us to see where and how we love. 'A queer liberation theology (or "indecent theology") needs to look for other love locations in the construction of the body in order to proceed with the disaffiliation necessary to allow an "original" body to emerge in theology' (Althaus-Reid, 2007c, p. 149). We need real bodies in love to craft theology. Loving our varied body parts and experiences expands our ways of knowing God.

Women's Bodies

It is particularly important to consider bodies because of the mutilation of women's bodies within the Christian tradition, beginning with Eve and Mary. In a book co-edited by Althaus-Reid and Lisa Isherwood,[1] entitled *Controversies in Body Theology*, they noted:

> We have chosen this title and this theme to create a reflective body theology in order to value and to love women's bodies ... What we have witnessed and experienced is a Christian culture that does indeed continue to slice the bodies of women through acts of theological dismemberment that begin with the fundamental split of mind from body. (Althaus-Reid and Isherwood, 2008, pp. 1–2)

For Althaus-Reid and Isherwood, we need to love our bodies, even those damaged by society and Christianity, starting by rejecting the split between body and soul. Christian theology has harmed women's bodies not only by prioritizing the soul over the body but also by denigrating women's bodies.

Unfortunately, throughout Christian theology, women have been harmed and excluded for not being male, not 'Adam'.

> In the meta-narrative of primordial sin, that 'Eve of destruction' of the scriptural narrative, a woman's body is signifier of that contract ... the woman does not exist as herself, she needs to be referred to and reminded of the illusion of an original or pure womanhood. (Althaus-Reid, 2008b, pp. 71–2)

Women have to be changed and purified because they are considered dirty as they naturally exist. Eve, the first woman, is blamed for all sinfulness, for example, although the story tells us Adam ate of the fruit. Somehow tradition decided that the 'tempting' was the actual problem not the partaking of the fruit of the tree, though that was what God prohibited.

Althaus-Reid offered several examples of the denigration of women's bodies in Christian tradition. 'Liturgically, the fact that women cover different parts of their bodies during mass has constituted a sign of the cosmetic cutting and reassembling of female bodies required in the separation of the sacred from the profane' (Althaus-Reid, 2008b, p. 77). Women have had to cover certain parts of their body in Christianity, even veiling their faces at one point. Althaus-Reid argues there is no one original body of a woman. Heterosexuality, patriarchy and Christianity have already changed women's bodies. It is for us to discover the sacred in our own bodies, to rescue them from Christianity's mutilation, and then decide whether and how we might want to change them.

Because the female body, more so than the white male body, has been denigrated, Althaus-Reid argued that female bodies can help us understand a different theology, one not based on heterosexuality and patriarchy. 'It seems that female bodies are then condemned to be permanent exteriorities, denouncing somehow the impossibility of heterosexuality' (Althaus-Reid, 2008b, pp. 76–7). Can women begin to consider what they want with and from their bodies, without the constraining framework of heterosexuality?

Althaus-Reid argued that theology has exiled bodies, particularly women's bodies. If traditional theology has excluded us, we can craft theology to include our ways of knowing God. 'As women, we know that we do not fit the constructions of the body that Christianity has provided us with. However, God does not fit them either' (Althaus-Reid, 2004d, p. 166). Women can move forward knowing that while the body assigned to them by theology is wrong, so too is the limited construction of God. Neither women nor God match their definitions.

Althaus-Reid highlighted the positive aspects of women's bodies in exile. 'First of all, cities of exile are places of liberative refuge, in the sense that the divine body becomes the original grounded "divine signifier", or the space in which to be *Other*' (Althaus-Reid, 2004d, p. 159). The exiled body is a refuge for the different. And this refuge can save us: 'There is a space of redemption to be found in the interstices between the place of God and women's bodies: such space makes of women's bodies a place of salvation' (Althaus-Reid, 2004d, p. 159). We can find new understandings of salvation in this exile. Further, in the sharing of the experiences of our bodies, we also restore a knowing of the divine. 'A woman's body, is "recreated" from the divine body in a movement of restoration; there is a giving back of the eucharist, or a return of gratitude, but only if we start with the body "as is"' (Althaus-Reid, 2004d, p. 159). Seeing our bodies as crafted in the image of God can help us to know God; our bodies as they are lead us to God.

For Althaus-Reid, focusing on women's bodies gives us both a resource for theology and a context for theologizing. 'What we are saying here is that a woman's body is simultaneously source and context in theology ... The woman's body is the grounded experience of our theological praxis and as such a space to be theologically de-colonised' (Althaus-Reid, 2004d, pp. 158–9). From our exiled bodies, new understandings of God and new theologies emerge, women's bodies in particular, beyond the bounds of colonialism, patriarchy and hetero-sexuality.

In particular, Althaus-Reid wanted us to understand women's bodies as sacred, though society does not. 'The body of the poor Latin American woman, malnourished, exposed to continuous pregnancies, violence and hunger speaks to us of the community which Christ came to save and for which he died, tortured and thirsty' (Althaus-Reid, 2004b, p. 45). Marginalized women's bodies in particular show us the failure of our treatment of others; further, it adds to the one male incarnation of God. We are all part of the body of Christ, not just the male Jesus.

Althaus-Reid celebrated Isherwood for her prioritization of the body in theology. 'She [Isherwood] pioneered a break-through in feminist theology by returning the body to Christian praxis ... The breakthrough produced by sexual feminist the-ologies represents, theologically, the return of the larger body or what we can call the "Six foot tall woman"' (Althaus-Reid, 2004d, pp. 162–3). This six-foot-tall woman refers to a science fiction film, where large women are feared, of course. Patriarchy fears real women, their bodies and their theology too. Theology also fears real women.

To highlight this subjugation and denigration of the body and the potential for new theologies, Althaus-Reid noted, 'Isher-wood reminds us of the sheer material exclusion of our bodies in theology ... We can talk about torture and salvation but not of vaginas and salvation' (Althaus-Reid, 2003b, pp. 188–9). Certain body parts are off-limits to traditional theology; we can work from them to craft new theologies.

Celebrating Body Parts

Could we begin to talk about God from body parts such as the vagina? 'In Isherwood ... The vagina is a theological locus to be privileged, as a place to be and to have, in order to start reflecting on God and the body "as is"' (Althaus-Reid, 2004d, p. 166). Where traditional theology has been phallic, women could begin from our own sexual loci, beginning to celebrate rather than hide our own body parts.

For Althaus-Reid, theology also ignores the hairy armpit, because hairy armpits refuse to follow the status quo. 'The fact is that beyond the domesticated, shaved bodies of patriarchal theology, and the politics of limits imposed on women's theological thinking, there are armpits with glorious, rebellious chestnut bushy hair shouting out loudly their different stories' (Althaus-Reid, 2004d, pp. 157–8). Women adhering to traditional theologies had shaved armpits; hairy armpits show resistance and difference. She uses a variety of imagery from 'imperfect' women, women who refuse to submit to patriarchal norms, to explore theological concepts.

Althaus-Reid wanted women's bodies to be in conversation with Christ to broaden the understanding of the incarnation and what bodily theology is. In exploring bodies, Althaus-Reid considered the example of a feetishist in Brazil, Mattoso. This artist invited people to kiss and touch the feet of workers,

> as a form of understanding issues of humiliation and arrogance by the exchange of places between the oppressor and the oppressed, producing a new synthesis of humiliation and power together with pleasure in the context of classist, heterosexist, and racist Brazilian society. (Althaus-Reid, 2007c, p. 135)

Not only did Mattoso draw attention to an under-focused area of the body, he also upended traditional roles whereby those with power served those without. For Althaus-Reid, one purpose of theology is to upend our traditional assumptions about God.

In these marginalized areas of our own bodies, indecent and queer theologies emerge, as the following chapters explore. 'Queer theologies are theosocial reflections that somehow feel at home with kissing the dirty feet of a worker, because the starting point of queering theology is always the body' (Althaus-Reid, 2007c, p. 136). Where traditional theologies tend to denigrate particular aspects of the body, Althaus-Reid wanted theology to begin from every part of the body; such theology is indecent and queer.

What we learn from bodies is that there is no one perfect body. It is altogether that we become one body of Christ, in all our sexual and gender differences.

> Transsexualism and transgenderism remind us that sexual identities can only be found grounded in earthquakes: their only commonality is their continuous and slippery *différence*. A woman's identity in the struggle against gender and sexual legitimacy systems requires subversive procedures, which could sometimes be cosmetic procedures … At the end, as we receive the body of Christ in the host, and Christ and ourselves merge, we are supposed to lose the illusion of identity in the midst of the Eucharist: the Divine requires a new nose and I require a sense of the divine. (Althaus-Reid, 2008b, p. 78)

Trans bodies, in particular, show us the spectrum of bodily changes as we all become part of Christ. Human and divine become merged, forming a new diverse body; we are all together the body of Christ, whatever our differences.

It is important to note and celebrate differences in individual bodies and experiences, and also celebrate the whole body of Christ that is only completely crafted with each of us. 'The divine body becomes a place in which we can become larger, one in which we are able to assume in solidarity the experiences of *anOther* body even when its experiences are alien to us' (Althaus-Reid, 2004d, p. 162). We come to know God as we come to know others in the body of Christ.

Unlike traditional theologies, which denigrated or ignored the body, Althaus-Reid wanted us to celebrate bodies as a way to know God. Every body part is included here, particularly those ignored previously. We begin with our real bodies to do real theologies, indecent and queer theologies, as the following chapters argue.

Suggested reading

Althaus-Reid, M., 2004d, '"Pussy, Queen of Pirates": Acker, Isherwood and the Debate on the Body in Feminist Theology', *Feminist Theology*, 12, pp. 157–67.

Althaus-Reid, M., 2007c, 'Feetishism: The Scent of a Latin American Body Theology', in Burrus, V. and C. Keller, eds, *Towards a Theology of Eros: Transfiguring Passion at the Limits of Discipline*, pp. 134–52, Fordham: Fordham University Press.

Althaus-Reid, M., 2008b, 'Mutilations and Restorations: Cosmetic Surgery in Christianity', in Althaus-Reid, M. and L. Isherwood, eds, *Controversies in Body Theology*, pp. 70–9, London: SCM Press.

Note

1 Lisa Isherwood is a British professor and feminist theologian, focusing on body theology.

9

Indecency/Decency

Decency was a controlling concept of life in Marcella's early years in Argentina. The government's imposition of decency on human beings (and thus indecency on people who refused to conform) informed her work and was the basis for her first book. For Marcella, indecency reopens the possibilities for knowing God.

Decency

Althaus-Reid titled her first book *Indecent Theology*. At the core of her analysis was the concept that traditional Christianity supports a dualism between decency and indecency. Traditional theology has argued that decent means Christian and indecent means sinful. Althaus-Reid challenged this dualism and the contents of this dualism, particularly its negative effects on women. Women have had to submit to this dominant harmful theology. The economy, church and political realm all rest on patriarchy, labelling women either decent when they conform or indecent when they resist.

Althaus-Reid noted that the Latin American experience with decency started with the colonizers imposing their concept of decency on the indigenous. 'Decency is a category brought to Latin America by the Conquistadors in the sixteenth century' (Althaus-Reid, 1996b, p. 136). The colonizers' concept of decency included the subordination of women in every realm. 'Decency as a theological category applies to the politics of what is considered proper, and the orderly state of things, in our lives as women and in our relation with God' (Althaus-

Reid, 1996b, p. 136). Decency controls proper behaviour in all realms. Only indecency can help us think outside this framework, which sees particular souls as more sinful than others.

This conception of decency, particularly for women, continued throughout Latin American history. 'Decency and indecency are two powerful conceptual regulators of women's lives. A decent woman ... is regulated and controlled by a complex series of spatial and time codes, including dressing, hours to be seen in the streets' (Althaus-Reid, 1996a, pp. 71–2). What a woman wears, what she can say, how she behaves are all controlled. In Argentina, decency became attached to patriotism. Women who struggled against the dictatorship or for the right to vote were indecent. Decency assumed that women were solely to be mothers, taking care of their children. Women concerned with anything outside of being a wife and mother were indecent, condemned religiously and politically.

Anything that disrupts the 'normal' heterosexual patriarchal order of the economy and the political realm is deemed indecent. 'From a distorted male spiritual conception, the political dissenters were seen as sexual deviants, that is homosexuals, lesbians or whores whereby their political actions were a menace to the size and power of the military ideology' (Althaus-Reid, 2000c, p. 186). From the dominant straight male perspective, criticizing politics was anti-heterosexual. Even critiquing the political realm excludes one from heterosexual decency. From this conception of decency/indecency, Althaus-Reid explored sexuality, as the following chapters detail.

Narrow dominant heterosexuality is construed as decent. Anything apart from one man and one woman in a marriage for life is indecent. 'Decency is the name of the Latin American closeted heterosexuality, that is, the assumption that even heterosexuality can be moulded according to a prescripted way – which is not true' (Althaus-Reid, 2000c, p. 46). Decent heterosexuality was based on an ideology not real relationships. Heterosexuality itself is experienced in myriad ways and relationships. Theology does not expand to consider these paths.

Women are deemed prostitutes when they behave indecently, whether or not women sell sex; the same is not true for men.

Christianity has exacerbated this process. Further, it 'has not changed men's sexuality based on men's alienation from their bodies and their association between sex and violence and no substantial challenges to capitalism or globalization processes can be done from there' (Althaus-Reid, 2004b, p. 90). While straight men need not change, any 'other' – women, homosexual, bisexual, etc. – does.

In sum, Althaus-Reid argued:

Decency/Indecency is a dialectical praxis based on the following elements:

1 that sex is a given, natural phenomenon. [So first, we assume there is one correct way to have a sex and to have sex.]
2 that God's sexual story according to the Christian Grand Narrative is normative.

Therefore, God has sex with young Mary without a meaningful relationship, and Jesus is conceived by male and not female desire. That sexual immaturity attributed to the Big God called 'the father' is extended to the portrayal of a Christ unable to understand or develop human sexuality in the context of a loving community of equals. (Althaus-Reid, 2004b, p. 85)

Second, normal sex involves God and Mary somehow without penetration, God fathers Jesus without Mary being involved in the conception, and Jesus doesn't have sex. What does that mean for our sex lives? In traditional theology, having sex has been deemed negative, even sinful.

Indecency: Deconstruction

Althaus-Reid reclaimed indecency as a positive and suggested it as a way to do theology, striving towards justice. 'By *indecenting* I mean a way of doing theology; a way to do a political and Queer Theology of belonging and becoming that is concerned with a gospel of justice ... indecenting is a way to unveil sexual ideologies in theology' (2011, p. 448). 'Indecenting' becomes a method to work towards a more just world. The point of indecent theology is both to deconstruct harmful 'decent' theology and to construct 'indecent' theologies.

Althaus-Reid taught us how to do indecent theology with: 'Clues for indecent practices in theology' (Althaus-Reid, 2005b, p. 35). First is 'Acknowledging the edges of the construction of the theological subject' (Althaus-Reid, 2005b, p. 35). Where have the borders been placed? What has theology allowed and what and who has theology excluded? Second is 'Acknowledging the relation between sexual ideologies and class and race ideologies; that is, seeing the relationships between poverty and sexuality' (Althaus-Reid, 2005b, p. 36). We need to address oppressions together, not separately, a mistake some liberation theologies have made. Third is 'Learning to engage in a theology of story, where people can "come out" as they are' (Althaus-Reid, 2005b, p. 36). We learn to know God by telling and hearing stories of our real lives. Fourth is 'Reading the Bible and our church traditions sexually' (Althaus-Reid, 2005b, p. 36). Sexuality is part of our lives; we should not read the biblical text as an asexual document. 'Finally, exploring themes of God and sexuality beyond heterosexual metaphors' (Althaus-Reid, 2005b, p. 36). Various sexualities are part of our lives, even for heterosexuals. Most people do not fit the narrow authoritative definition of heterosexuality. Indecenting is a starting point in overcoming the gap.

The task is difficult. '*Indecenting* as a method takes courage. It requires unfaithfulness to ideologies and honesty with God. At least it requires some discernment in terms of where our faithfulness lies' (Althaus-Reid, 2011, p. 450). Indecent theology requires us to examine what we have been taught, subjecting it all to suspicion, and be honest about our own experiences.

It should be obvious then that Christianity and patriarchy have gone together. Decent sexuality goes with decent economics, decent politics and decent religion. We need to undo decency, 'By subverting, or making indecent that ideological sacralization of a sexual economic oppressive construct which kills women and makes them into the fetish of a disconnected ontology and an exploitative form of production' (Althaus-Reid, 2004b, p. 87). Post-feminists and indecent theologians unmask the theology and ideology that harms women. Althaus-Reid wanted us to subject these norms that denigrate women and sexual 'others' to suspicion.

Indecency analyses sexuality, as it exists on the ground, not as ideologically presented. It works from real lives and experiences.

> Indecent Theology is an attempt to reflect on the interrelation between theological and political discourses from the perspective of a Sexual Theology, centered on the intimate connections between the sexual and socio-political hegemonic constructions to be found at the base of Capitalism. (Althaus-Reid, 1998c, p. 4)

Indecent theology examines connections between sex, economics, politics and religion. While liberation theology challenged many assumptions of capitalism, it did not challenge patriarchy or heterosexuality, partly due to its failure to use a post-colonial analysis. 'What the colonial masters made illegal for native men and for their society in terms of economic organization, jurisprudence, religious and educational structure, for women and for those of other sexual orientations it was termed indecent' (Althaus-Reid, 1998c, p. 4). Decency is legal, controlling women and non-heterosexuals; indecency is illegal. Men and women both were subjected to heterosexual norms, norms whereby women were subservient to men. We need to re-examine these norms. Heterosexuality still underlies our religious, economic and political realms.

Indecency dislocates theology as it stands; heterosexual patriarchal theology is limited and wrong, particularly in its claim to be normative. 'This [indecent theology] is a theology the main function of which is to destabilize the decent order, that is a constructed political, social and sexual order which has been ideologically sacralised' (Althaus-Reid, 2004e, p. 25).

Indecent theology aims to deconstruct the harms of decency. The goal is to upend normative dominant structures, to enable diverse alternatives.

For Althaus-Reid, indecent theology expands on feminist and liberation theologies. It openly explores sexualities, rather than ignoring them. Indecency recognizes sex as a part of all aspects of our lives. Our sexual self is not cut off from the remainder of life. 'No matter what metaphor you use, theology has been and will remain a sexual praxis ... Theological Mono-loving is carried through political and economical frames of thought ... the association between monotheism, monarchism and the subjection of women' (Althaus-Reid, 2004e, p. 100). Traditional theology has been all about sex, although negatively and only rarely directly mentioned; even the love of the one God is set within a particular heterosexual, political and economic construct.

Indecent theology aims to do theology from a poor woman's perspective, so long ignored in Latin America and beyond. 'My own queer project of "indecenting" theology has been an attempt to destabilize the complexity of theology, feminism and identity when it relates to native women and to open doors to doing a feminist Latin American liberation theology' (Althaus-Reid, 2008a, p. 110). Indecent theology first recognizes the ways that theology labels and excludes women, finding new ways to speak theologically from the experiences of women. 'The "theology part" of feminist liberation theology needed to stabilize the woman native as subject of theology in order that the theological identity could be stabilized ... Urban poor women tend to subvert the theological place' (Althaus-Reid, 2008a, p. 111). Theology aimed to control and stabilize but women and non-heterosexuals destabilize theology. Theology directed towards women has been from a male perspective, to uphold straight male dominance. Even where women have a place, theology prioritizes decent women over other women.

It is indecent simply to begin theology from the marginalized. Second, it is indecent to unmask the ideologies that exist in our theologies.

If we want to pursue an Indecent Theology, and to indecent God, we must start first by analyzing how theology can
perform as an imperial sexual act ... Theology is an art per
se, that is an aesthetic representation and not a natural but
a naturalized way of reflecting/acting on God and people.
(Althaus-Reid, 2000c, p. 92)

Theology can only be a partial reflection of God. Theology needs
to recognize the aspects of sexuality it carries with it. We need
to expose harmful theology and change it. Even in theology,
Althaus-Reid noted, while one can ask whether or not God
exists, one cannot ask how our sexuality might expand. In fact,
one is prevented from being honest about sexual experiences.

Indecency: Construction

Starting this theological journey, Althaus-Reid argued, begins
with 'indecent exposures', that is, 'expanding the sexual
borders of the properly theologically dressed women, thus
becoming indecent theologians' (Althaus-Reid, 2000b, p. 219).
Indecency begins to think theologically from real experiences.
'Indecency is ... the reality of our experience which does not
match and cannot validate the faith as ideology in which we
have been brought up. Indecency is subversive' (Althaus-Reid,
1996b, p. 136). Indecency shows us that our realities and our
frameworks do not match; hence, we need to prioritize reality.
'Indecent theology challenges the organic assumptions in our
theological and economic structures built around the belief in
functions of obedience' (Althaus-Reid, 1998c, p. 10). Rather
than craft theology and then repeatedly fail to enact it, since it
does not relate to reality, we should begin with our realities,
analysing how we relate to God.
    Indecency aims to expand theology, moving beyond dualistic
notions, but this is a difficult process. It is easier to deconstruct
than to find new constructions. 'The commonality between
post-colonialism and indecent hermeneutics is that women do
not claim essentialism and neither does the colonial subject ...

However ... we do not have a women's language or a women's alternative system to refer to' (Althaus-Reid, 2004b, pp. 84–5). We want to craft alternatives, not one but many. The trouble we face is that indecency has been defined by decency, women have been defined by men. The goal is not to formulate a new authoritative women's theology but to bring to light new theologies in all their diversity. What is called normative is actually not the experience of many people; it represents an ideology rather than reality.

Althaus-Reid continued that the point is not to craft a new authoritative theology or a new authoritative sexuality. Replacing heterosexuality with homosexuality would not solve the underlying problem of having one dominant framework. 'Sexuality per se, as in sexual knowledge, does not bring salvation unless there is a serious challenge to the heteronormativity of past theologies' (Althaus-Reid, 2003b, pp. 187–8). The point is to allow varying theologies and sexualities to emerge.

Indecency both transgresses traditional theology and progresses. Hence, this theology is a process without an end. 'Indecent Theology is also a caminata, and to continue walking in this theological praxis requires us to forgo any claimed stability: we must be prepared to accept challenges and self-evaluation' (Althaus-Reid, 2004b, p. 64). The key is to continue the spiral of actions and reflections.

Indecenting theology, for Althaus-Reid, was her attempt to understand God despite varying oppressions. 'My theological upbringing made me understand reality, God and society critically. Therefore, the pain of love was also related to poverty, and sexuality to economy' (Althaus-Reid, 2003b, p. 182). She saw connections between love, poverty, political oppression and religious oppression. In order to understand God, we must first realize that we have not yet fully understood and that what purports to be authoritative is at best a partial knowing. Instead, we need 'a diasporic theology ... that affirms and supports new theological identities in Christianity ... nondocility towards established bodies of theological knowledge or orthodoxia' (Althaus-Reid, 2003b, p. 183). We should not submit to any system without questioning.

Althaus-Reid wanted indecency to forget about the 'normal' and focus on the real, celebrating reality.

> By taking on board the concept of indecency in Latin America as a positive, subversive one, the concept of normality is also challenged ... Indecent Theology is produced by that element of sexual dissidence, rooted in class analysis and the reality of the life of the poor in an urban mega-city such as Buenos Aires, mixed with the complexities of issues of race, sexuality, economic exclusion. (Althaus-Reid, 2004b, p. 63)

Indecent becomes a positive term, reflecting real life. This new theology begins from the margins, as the margins actually are, not as liberationists hoped they would be. This theology should remain at the margins, with the marginalized. It should not try to become authoritative and systematic (Althaus-Reid, 2004b, p. 64). Rather than try to adjust previous theology, we need to begin anew from the excluded.

Indecent theology is a celebratory theology, rejecting harmful concepts and supporting women and all 'others'. We can celebrate the positive experiences of women's sex lives while trying to enable further positive experiences. The point is to see and celebrate diversity. It is to see the varying realities and how they help us to understand God, not to form one particular reality. In contrast to a systematic theology, real theologies doubt ideology, speaking from realities. Varieties of theologies will emerge, helping us to better know each other and God.

An indecent theology asks us to craft an anthropology based on women's perspectives (Althaus-Reid, 2004b, p. 88). First, we need to explore women's sexualities. Expanding the concept of sexuality also means that we recognize economies, sexuality and faith are intertwined. Second, we need to do research based on real women, sexual research that informs our theology. Women's experiences need to form the basis for theologies, and theology should celebrate women, not denigrate them. Finally, we 'need to disentangle women from the sufferings produced by the theological confusion created between love and sexuality, which makes love more important for women's fulfilment than sex, and ends making love and sexuality synonymous' (Althaus-Reid, 2004b, pp. 88–9). We need to consider all types of love, not just agape, and how to enable women to celebrate their various experiences of loving.

This theology expands the work of liberation theologies, aiming to bring us towards a better understanding of God and each other. 'My path ... is a path from the margins of sexual and economic exclusion towards an understanding of a larger Jesus, a greater God and an infinitely wider Christianity' (Althaus-Reid, 2004b, p. 4). Indecent theology works towards justice in loving relationships. Rather than narrowing our notions of God, Jesus and the Holy Spirit, Althaus-Reid urges us to expand them.

Christology obviously begins with Jesus Christ but it does not end with the four Gospel narratives or 'church' interpretations. 'The Christological process starts not with the first meetings of church councils but with the construction of the Christ ... a process that depends on the interrelationship between a man called Jesus and a community of women, men and children' (Althaus-Reid, 2004b, p. 83). We can indecent Christ to re-imagine Christology and see how Jesus lived and loved and how we live and love. As noted in the chapter critiquing liberation and feminist theologies, Althaus-Reid argued that Christ should be able to be seen as a child prostitute. Why would we refuse this image? Where might we have unfairly limited our Christologies? In the conversation about Jesus, it will not simply be about what Jesus did, but what women tell us about Jesus, from their experiences. Our lives and Jesus' life speak to each other. Jesus never experienced being female; women can add this aspect.

Queering is also a form of indecency, as following chapters will highlight. The idea is to see what might be possible rather than work from or towards fixed ideas. Formalizing the ideas goes against both notions. For example, the idea is not to create one new Virgin Mary but to expose the Marys that currently exist. Every aspect of Christianity needs to be subjected to suspicion, and new aspects celebrated as they emerge.

Suggested reading

Althaus-Reid, M., 2000c, 'Introduction', in *Indecent Theology: Theological Perversions in Sex, Gender and Politics*, pp. 1–9, New York: Routledge.

Althaus-Reid, M., 2003b, 'On Non-Docility and Indecent Theologians: A Response to the Panel for Indecent Theology', *Feminist Theology*, 11, pp. 182–9.

Althaus-Reid, M., 2004b, 'Introduction to Part Two', in *From Feminist Theology to Indecent Theology*, pp. 61–4, London: SCM Press.

10

Heterosexuality

For Althaus-Reid, it is not gender or class or race at the basis of the dominant constructs. Instead, each of these emerges from a heterosexual framework. Althaus-Reid's work deconstructed heterosexuality in economics and theology through a bisexual lens. Her work detailed how the rejection of other sexualities has framed patriarchy and dominated the capitalist system and Christian theology. She suggested enabling alternatives instead of one dominant framework.

The Dominance of Heterosexuality

Heterosexuality, narrowly defined, is closely linked with decency, as the previous chapter explored. Many heterosexuals do not neatly fit the assigned frame. One can see this emphasis on heterosexuality in the dictatorship in Argentina. Anything considered wrong is condemned as non-heterosexual. Heterosexuality dominates the discussion and enforces its behaviours without representing reality. Dominant heterosexuality created a narrow frame of existence and claimed it as normative. Patriarchy relies on heterosexuality. 'Heterosexuality is a concept that denounces more clearly the dualistic conceptions of the patriarchal system with a boldness which allows us to remember what is at the base of our experiences of reality' (Althaus-Reid, 1997, p. 46). Rather than focus on equality between the sexes, we should question the notion of fixed sexuality.

Heterosexuality focuses on male desire of women, although it enforces only having sex within marriage between one man and one woman. 'Male desire is perpetuated through the interrelation of three elements ... an allegiance amongst men to perpetuate patriarchy, and also by the regulation of homophobia and misogyny ... always reflecting two sexual structures of oppression – marriage and heterosexuality' (Althaus-Reid, 2000c, p. 89). Straight male desire exerts control through patriarchy, heterosexuality and denigration of women. While heterosexuality claims to focus on male/female marriage, the woman exists for male desire, companionship and reproduction.

Heterosexuality, with its dualistic relationships between men and women, orders our economy, society and political realm, including our theology. The dualism enables heterosexual theology to condemn what is outside, while supporting only what is inside. Althaus-Reid offered several examples of how non-heterosexuals are denigrated in order to support and promote heterosexuality. In the biblical text, she notes 'women, and sexual dissidents in general, are merely depicted for the consumption of a constructed male heterosexual reader' (Althaus-Reid, 2000c, p. 93). When 'others' emerge in the text, they serve as foils for the heterosexual male. This narrow spectrum of heterosexuality is defined more by what it is not rather than what it is. In this way, it subsumes everyone to its laws. We need to move beyond such dualisms.

Analysing heterosexuality in its historical context shows us, according to Althaus-Reid, that Christianity was bound up with heterosexuality and enforced heterosexuality on the Latin American continent rather than teaching Christian theology itself (Althaus-Reid, 2003c, p. 9). 'Issues of monogamy, heterosexual marriage and gender codes, treated according to the European prevalent fashion, had such a pre-eminence in the teaching of the church that ... the Christian mission seemed to depend on sexuality' (Althaus-Reid, 2007b, p. 128). The church focused on heterosexual marriage and patriarchy, denigrating other experiences as sinful. Christianity often ends up prescribing particular behaviours rather than enabling people to engage theology from their own perspectives, or even to learn why particular rules exist.

Heterosexual Theology

Christianity supported a narrow version of heterosexuality. 'Monotheism, monogamy, and the global order are concepts closely linked together' (Althaus-Reid, 1997, p. 49). Traditional theology was built on an ideal that negates sexuality, rather than the realities of our sex lives. It focuses on a hegemony of narrow heterosexual behaviour.

> Classical theology has been built as a highly sexual theology with an inner logic of attraction. Its values, beliefs, objectives and strategies are all of a deeply heterosexual nature, telling us how to attract love from God but not how to be, and to feel/live that of God in us. (Althaus-Reid, 1997, p. 50)

Theology is more about controlling what we believe through heterosexuality than about how we actually experience God's love. Theology purports to include everyone, but the messages tend to prioritize heterosexual men and be written by heterosexual men. Other desires lie outside the system, condemned. Heterosexuality and Christianity tend to prioritize male desire, but narrow male desire for one woman.

Liberation theology too normalized heterosexuality. At best, liberation theology tolerates other sexualities; however, its framework is based on a heterosexual ideal. Early liberationists argued that heterosexuality was key to liberation theology. 'Early in the 1970s, Enrique Dussel produced a sophisticated political condemnation of non-heterosexuality which gave rise to non-heterosexual desires becoming part of a theological reflection on structures of sin' (Althaus-Reid, 2009b, p. 10). For Dussel,[1] difference is important to liberation theology; heterosexuality enshrines difference, while homosexuality valorizes the same. According to Dussel:

> The capitalist system is characterized by a rejection of alternatives and Otherness. The face of the Other, of the poor and vulnerable in society, is excluded and denied ... reduced to a thing ... A capitalist system ... is a project of Sameness. (Althaus-Reid, 2009b, p. 11)

Capitalism prioritizes self over others, treating others as objects rather than people. Dussel saw the nuclear family as key to liberation, if reformed. For Dussel, the nuclear family itself is composed correctly, as the basis of community. 'Curiously, he attacks homosexuality and feminism as "a negation of sexual diversity"(Dussel, 1977, p. 101)' (Althaus-Reid, 2009b, p. 12). For Dussel, patriarchy was wrong but true heterosexual relations could fix it; homosexuality was excluded.

Other liberationists held this perspective on homosexuality, as selfish and anti-communal. 'Another liberationist argument ... was that homosexuality is an egoist act ... denying the sacrificial givenness of oneself in a family, orientated to the production of children. Homosexuality was ... partaking of the capitalist ideological standpoint of domination' (Althaus-Reid, 2009b, p. 12). Homosexuality reinforced capitalism's ideal of selfishness. Liberationists rejected the possibility of loving the same sex, considering it part of a capitalist system, prioritizing one's own desires over continuing the community.

Althaus-Reid was critical of the idea that homosexuality should be 'accepted' into the dominant systems. She asked:

> Are we being swallowed into the old colonial mechanism of accepting the declared 'abnormal' ... into the heterosexual normality? ... The churches would end by openly ordaining and marrying lesbigays in the same way that in the sixteenth century the Pope finally accepted that Latin Americans have souls ... Why does something need to be accepted? Because it belongs to the domains of the Other to the non-context which cannot be eliminated sometimes but is exploited. (Althaus-Reid, 1997, p. 47)

Inclusion aims to absorb the abnormal into the normal, if it will agree to assimilate. Rather than actually change in the face of diversity, it tries to include and absorb. The issue of inclusion arose around same-sex marriage, which, while enabling any two people to marry, unfortunately left intact the model of marriage between two individuals as the basis of community.

Heterosexual theologies struggle because they are not based on the realities of life. 'Heterosexual theology has found in its development the same problems and difficulties that people usually find in their sexual lives, for instance, issues of hierarchical relations, positioned bodies and monogamic patterns of thought' (Althaus-Reid, 2000c, p. 88). Heterosexual theologies are in constant tension with reality; they focus on ideologies of hierarchy and normative behaviours. Althaus-Reid referred to examples of theologians whose sex lives were divorced from their theological output, for example Paul Tillich's love of sadomasochism and bondage.[2] For Althaus-Reid, the problem is not that Tillich was attracted to bondage but that he failed to consider this theologically. 'Our difficulty with Tillich is his lack of integrity ... God cannot be Queered unless theologians have the courage to come out from their homosexual, lesbian, bisexual, transgendered, transvestite or (ideal) heterosexual closets' (Althaus-Reid, 2000c, p. 88). Tillich's theology may have been different if he honestly considered his sexual desires. If I theologize from a dishonest basis, I cannot know God. I either limit my experiences of God or lie about them.

Even within heterosexual relationships there is a great diversity unexplored within the framework of dominant heterosexual narratives. Heterosexuality aims to provide a stable society through marriage, limiting external relationships. Adultery is just one example of this attempt to break from the narrow definition of one man and one woman in partnership for life. There are many examples of how heterosexuality tries to define reality. This dominant framework also promotes secrecy among those who choose different paths, and their exclusion from the 'norm'.

The first step is to question the 'normalization' of heterosexuality. 'First, a suspicion concerning the assumption that heterosexuality is a universal and stable sexual identity and as such part of a natural (sacralized) order' (Althaus-Reid, 2008c, p. 91). Dominant heterosexuality is an ideology not matching reality. The next step is to recognize that this 'normalization' leads to oppression. 'Second, the realization of the fact that hegemonic constructions of sexual identity have historically contributed to the consolidation of oppressive structures of power relationships in the Christian Church and in theology' (Althaus-Reid, 2008c, p. 91). Christianity consolidated power through supporting patriarchal heterosexuality. It oppresses many people through its idealization of heterosexuality, heterosexuals included.

We know that not all men and women are heterosexual, for example, or if heterosexual may want different loving relationships.

> From ... poor women in Latin America we hear about the desire to love other women, and ... how peaceful an experience it is for women harassed in the *machista's* Latin American system. Dreams of having more than one man, of loving different men also express the need to cease to be sexual property and grow sexually. (Althaus-Reid, 2004b, p. 93)

Latin American women who love other women, or who partner with more than one man, express enjoying freedom from some aspects of male domination. These varying examples of loving can expand our notion of a loving God.

Rather than assume sexual identity as something natural, we can recognize that it is political. We can consider other sexualities within themselves, for themselves, not compared to heterosexuality. 'Moreover, if homosexuality is a category invented by and grounded on heterosexual understandings, it may carry within itself characteristics of heterosexual thinking' (Althaus-Reid, 2008c, p. 92). Homosexuality, for example, is defined in contrast to heterosexuality, rather than in and of itself. Althaus-Reid used the concept of sodomy to explore differing relations in theology (Althaus-Reid, 2000c, pp. 194–5). The negativity around sodomy was its failure to reproduce; it related men to other men rather than men to women. In such a dualistic framework, this meant one man was submissive to another, interrupting patriarchal relations. Rather than seeing homosexual relations as an area in which ways of relating could be rethought, it was assumed one partner would be masculine and the other feminine. But what would homosexuality add or change about theology, if not defined in heterosexual patriarchal terms?

Beyond Heterosexuality

What alternatives might there be to a dominant heterosexual narrative? Note the plural. The goal for Althaus-Reid was not to denigrate heterosexuality in favour of another form of sexuality. We should destabilize any 'normative' framework. Referring to the Trinity, she noted God's multiple relationships. The notion of the Trinity offers us a variety of possible relationships, expanding rather than limiting our frameworks.

> The point is to ask whether by opening up the hidden relationships of each person of the Trinity we might not destabilize power through desire and knowledge ... The difficulty for heterosexuality is to grasp the fact that not all sex has a name or a date or place of discovery. (Althaus-Reid, 2003c, pp. 58–9)

How do God, Jesus and the Holy Spirit love? We do not need boxes for sexuality or God.

When we share our own experiences we realize the shallowness of connection to God within dominant heterosexuality. 'Reflecting on our sexual stories, we can find the narratives of production imposed on us by heterosexuality at economic, social, political and religious levels' (Althaus-Reid, 1997, p. 49). Opening up about how experiences differ from the 'norm', is the first step. 'The main issue is to take the problematizing of our private pain out of the closet, because women's pain is collective, massive pain, and remembering that nobody will leave this land of bondage ... on her own' (Althaus-Reid, 1997, p. 52). Telling our stories of suffering together can help free us from the thrall of the dominant systems; it can help us to find alternatives.

Althaus-Reid analysed Scripture from the perspective of heterosexuality to see where a heterosexual perspective has hidden other interpretations. The goal here is not solely to condemn the text but to see what is in the text. How can we celebrate difference in the face of the heterosexual violence in some of the texts? Reading the text from different perspectives gives us different experiences of the text and of our realities.

She analysed stories of Rahab and Lot in particular. The heterosexuality in these texts is violent, particularly against women. 'There is no point in denying the fact that this text is saturated with violence. Men from Sodom against these particular visitors; a father against his own daughters, and God against almost everybody and everything' (Althaus-Reid, 2003c, p. 91). Men and God exhibit violent behaviour against the different and against women. This heterosexual violence occurs throughout biblical texts; it must be interrogated rather than accepted. The men of God in the text began the violence. This narrative appears to tell us that this God prioritizes sameness over diversity. Violence is considered a positive to destroy this diversity, continuing even after Sodom and Gomorrah are destroyed.

> The scenes after the destruction of Sodom speak for themselves: a woman who refuses to forget that life was different … In this she acted like the mothers of the Plaza de Mayo who dared to commit the maximum offence that a person can do against a fascist system, which is to remember and to challenge the false memories. (Althaus-Reid, 2003c, p. 93)

Not only is the woman who wants to remember the past punished, but Lot's daughters are punished too, sexually assaulted. Reading from the underside, Lot's God does wrong, oppressing others, women in particular.

Althaus-Reid also interrogated the text of Rahab from the perspective of dominant heterosexuality. 'Rahab declares herself heterosexual … dis-assembles herself from what we have called the Sodomite culture, from her religion and values … declaring mono-fidelity to the mono-God of the foreigners – she saves herself from being sacrificed and gives that place to her nation' (Althaus-Reid, 2003c, pp. 104–5). Rahab saves herself and sends her community to death, instead becoming faithful to one God. Difference is obliterated. This same violent approach to difference occurred with colonization. Could we imagine Rahab behaving differently? Why does the heterosexual narrative require betrayal and violence? The God of Israel appears to support dominance and heterosexuality in these texts.

Althaus-Reid wanted to challenge theology with a bisexual approach. Althaus-Reid chooses to highlight bisexuality because, for her, it rejected the dualism of the heterosexual system, thinking more in terms of process rather than fixity. 'It is only bisexuality which displaces and causes tension to the established heterosexual dyad implicit in the theologian's identity and task' (Althaus-Reid, 2003c, p. 15). Bisexuality rejects the opposition of heterosexuality/homosexuality, introducing a spectrum of sexualities.

Women, for example, can challenge dominant heterosexuality's inadequacy through a bisexual lens. 'A woman has more than one point of becoming. The girl may be one, but menopause is other. Moreover, menopause may be even more crucial as it is uncharted territory for most women, and posits specific theological questions' (Althaus-Reid, 2008a, pp. 112–13). Women become all throughout their lives, not just once; life is a progression. Second, the woman should adopt a bisexual perspective, actually thinking through what and who she might desire, as a process rather than a fact. 'The girl needs to become the bi/girl … going through the transition, not defining her own sexual identity with respect to a centred definition of heterosexual hegemony' (Althaus-Reid, 2008a, p. 113). Our own desires shift and change throughout our lives. Third is rejecting finality, focusing on becoming. Althaus-Reid argued, 'the girl needs to become a theological writing strategy … to write queer theology as a transition' (Althaus-Reid, 2008a, p. 113). The notion of a spectrum changes sexuality into a process rather than a fact. Queer and indecent theologies then introduce other locations and people into the discussion, offering alternatives, not narrowing to one definition.

Althaus-Reid highlighted the normalcy of bisexuality in various indigenous traditions. For example, she discusses the town of Moya where bisexuality is an important part of the community. The town is surrounded by three divine mountains, one of which is bisexual, Apu Yaya. 'In the Andean context the category of intermediary has been dismissed in favour of allowing bisexuals to claim their own unique identity outside the mediation role of heterosexuality' (Althaus-Reid, 2003c, pp. 118–19). The mountains are important to daily life, showing a spectrum of sexuality. 'We could say that the Apu Yaya disrupts the privacy of the relationship between believers and the other masculine gods by providing hospitality by inclusion in itself' (Althaus-Reid, 2003c, p. 120). In this context, bisexuality counters dualism, forming a triad. In contrast to the Christian tradition, the Moya tradition actively includes bisexuality. What would Christian theology look like if it rejected the narrow framework of heterosexuality, if it contained a fluid conception of gender, sex and sexuality? There are, for example, three aspects of the Trinity, as there are three divine mountains in this community. 'The ethical values which inform the life of the community (which come from their bisexual understanding) are those of reciprocity and exchange as a form of re-distribution' (Althaus-Reid, 2003c, p. 122). Bisexuality helps to expose the problem of hierarchy inherent in patriarchy and heterosexuality.

Trinity

The Trinity could also help us to think beyond heterosexuality. God relates to Godself as a trio rather than a heterosexual partnership. Bisexuality or omnisexuality helps us understand the multiplicity of God. Bisexuality moves beyond dualism, as does the Trinity. Multiple relationships and types of relationships exist within God and also between ourselves and God.

God, the Holy Spirit and Jesus are dynamic, not fixed. For example, Althaus-Reid asked, 'Does the Trinitarian formula, made of repetition and complementarities, somehow express a second desire in the sense that God cannot be contained in Godself anymore?' (Althaus-Reid, 2004a, p. 399). God may not be satisfied with Godself. God becoming Jesus suggests God needed or wanted to expand and change, to interact with humanity in different ways.

How has our limited perspective on sexuality limited our understanding of God and our relationships with each other and with God?

> To claim that there are sexual irregularities in that translation of God in Jesus implies then that sexuality forces us to rethink not only the biological underpinnings of current theology, but also that sexuality makes us reflect on the sacred and the sexual gestures of legitimization behind the gendered and sexual dressings of God. (Althaus-Reid, 2004a, p. 399)

The way we dress the Trinity as patriarchal and heterosexual limits our notions of God, economics and other systems. Rethinking sexuality can help us to rethink our systems, all framed from dominant heterosexuality.

God has been assumed to be heterosexual and male. Yet, God is supposed to be neither male nor female; hence, God cannot be heterosexual. Yet, challenging the heterosexuality of God is taboo. Why wouldn't God be able to express a variety of sexualities? 'The desexualization of God ignores that sexual representations are at the core of any meaningful representation system, be it judicial, political or theological' (Althaus-Reid, 2000b, p. 217). Saying God is neither male nor female does not help us if we also deny God's sexuality. It removes rather than creates.

In considering God as a female prostitute, Althaus-Reid deliberately countered this asexuality. She asked, 'What is it in the life and sufferings of a poor prostitute (female or male) that the current theological representation of God cannot cope with? ... The "closedness" or short-circuit of heterosexual representation systems' (Althaus-Reid, 2000b, p. 215). God the prostitute does not fit into the ideal heterosexual system and so is excluded from consideration. Our understanding of God and theology have been limited, limiting our relationships with God.

Indecent and queer theologies want to read sacred text from perspectives other than formal heterosexuality. One beginning is to examine who Jesus developed relationships with. How did he work outside the box of his time? Althaus-Reid asked us to consider a bisexual Christ. What would it mean for Christology for Christ to be bisexual? 'In a Christology of a Bi/Christ we are considering two things: First, the reality of people's identity outside heterosexualism, and second, a pattern of thought for a larger Christ outside binary boundaries' (Althaus-Reid, 2000c, p. 117). The goal here is to release Jesus Christ from a narrow dualistic heterosexuality. The goal is not to redefine Christ in one way but to see Christ in many ways. Further, theologies assumed that Jesus was heterosexual but did not ever act sexually. Why would Jesus be limited in this way? Perhaps Jesus combined multiple human possibilities. Nothing is stated in the text about Jesus' sexuality.

Althaus-Reid wanted us to see how heterosexuality has been at the base of much oppression, including within the Christian tradition. Rejecting this narrow framework, she suggested bisexuality as a way to expand our understanding of God and theology. We need to let ourselves and God out of the closet. The following chapter discusses how 'queering' helps us to do so.

Suggested reading

Althaus-Reid, M., 1997, 'Sexual Strategies in Practical Theology: Indecent Theology and the Plotting of Desire with Some Degree of Success', *Theology and Sexuality*, 7, pp. 45–52.

Althaus-Reid, M., 2008a, 'The Bi/girl Writings: From Feminist Theology to Queer Theologies', in Isherwood, L. and K. McPhillips, eds, *Post-Christian Feminism: A Critical Approach*, pp. 105–16, Aldershot: Ashgate Publishing.

Althaus-Reid, M., 2009b, '"Let Them Talk …!" Doing Liberation Theology from Latin American Closets', in Althaus-Reid, M., ed., *Liberation Theology and Sexuality*, pp. 5–18, London: SCM Press.

Notes

1 Enrique Dussel (1934–) is an Argentinian liberation philosopher.
2 Paul Tillich (1886–1965) was a German-American Lutheran theologian.

II

Queering

Rather than create a stable systematic theology, Marcella argued that to begin to know God it was critical to queer God and theology. In particular, she argued for moving beyond the binary, emphasizing the denigrated to undo the hierarchy. Queering is the process of questioning all that has come before, examining real life at the margins of society and sexuality to find God.

Queer/ing

Queering as a method emerged from queer theory. 'Queer theory implies a hermeneutics of suspicion and a distrust of fixed identities' (Althaus-Reid, 2006b, pp. 52). Queer theory began with sexuality, questioning what was deemed the 'norm'. Citing Judith Butler,[1] Althaus-Reid states:

> Butler says that it is in the construction of heterosexuality that the three elements of sexuality (a practice), gender (a behaviour) and sex (a biological given) are supposed to combine in a biological destiny ... Queer theory would ... claim that in reality, gender, sexuality and sex seldom match each other. (Althaus-Reid, 2006b, p. 52)

While heterosexuality says that sex, gender and sexuality match, they often do not. Queering celebrates diversity rather than adhering to a narrow norm that does not match reality. Where society would prefer neat divisions and associations, reality is messy.

In terms of sexuality, queer theory articulated the spectrum of sexuality rather than sit within a dualism. Second, it acknowledged diversity within each sexual label, like hetero-sexuality. 'Third, it argued that sexuality, like gender, is taught and rehearsed' (Althaus-Reid, 2008c, p. 90). We can learn and unlearn sexuality, and express our sexuality in a wide variety of ways.

Queer theory and theology re-appropriate queer as a positive term. 'The term "queer", originally a term of abuse, has been appropriated in a positive sense in order to lay the stress on elements of unconventionality, nonconformity, and disruption' (Althaus-Reid, 2008c, pp. 89). To queer is to disrupt any norm. First, queer is a chosen location and stance. Second, this stance is suspicious of the framework of what is deemed normal. Third, queering aims to upend what is assumed to be normal. 'To queer, then, is to facilitate a process of leaving an assigned space of belonging' (Althaus-Reid, 2006b, p. 256). It is to reject a label and work towards alternatives, moving outside binaries.

Queer/ing Theologies

Althaus-Reid articulated queering theology as outing, arguing that theology has traditionally forced us into a closet; queer-ing continues the work of indecency. The important change in both these theologies is from trying to advance one theology to understanding there are many theologies. Queering theology relies on the experiences of the marginalized to produce alter-native understandings.

> Queer theology is the result of a broad alliance of methods and historical praxis of liberation which come from people outside hetero-patriarchy. The relation between construc-tions of sexuality, hegemonic thought and political/economic power are disclosed in Queer theology as part of a strategy for a real radical and alternative way of thinking and practis-ing God among us. (Althaus-Reid, 2001b, pp. 57–8)

Queer theology frees us to work beyond the hegemony of the powerful. By exposing how theology, heterosexuality and other systems have colluded to put us into boxes, we can begin to rethink our systems based on our realities.

Unlike theologies of the past, the aim is not to sell or promote. Instead it is to unpack and examine dominating frameworks. One particular theological concept that Althaus-Reid challenged, as we previously articulated, is redemption. 'As Queer Theologians, we are against the grain of the normal, and in this case, against Redemption as an economic metaphor for salvation' (Althaus-Reid, 2007d, p. 292). Theologies have told people that they are in debt to God because of their misbehaviour and that while we can never erase this debt, we can be saved. Queering theology thinks about salvation and our relationship with God differently.

We begin with love in all its forms. How does God love us? How do we love God? We can begin to understand God through love and thus re-understand notions of grace and redemption. 'Grace is the work of freeing and delivering people and nature for free: conversion, the transformation of a person into a great lover of justice, equality and peace' (Isherwood and Althaus-Reid, 2004, p. 2). God freely gives grace to transform us to work towards justice. This process of understanding salvation begins with loving relationships. Althaus-Reid noted that this process may be considered demonology by the traditional order, which has seen everything outside its narrow framework as demonic and wrong. 'Redemption can therefore be considered a coming out, an expansive experience and not just a retention of traditions' (Althaus-Reid, 2003c, p. 139). We redeem ourselves through honest reflection, through coming out. Althaus-Reid argued that we need to continue expanding our notions rather than limiting them.

The goal is to find our actual souls and how we connect to God, not the souls and relationships that we were sold. In doing so, we begin to better understand ourselves, each other and God. 'We may be doing a theology of encountering strangers, including a stranger God and a Queer Messiah, but in the end, Queering theology brings us back to ourselves, to our own lost soul' (Althaus-Reid, 2004e, p. 34). For Althaus-Reid, redemption may simply mean understanding ourselves. 'It is curious, and *queer*, to discover that, paradoxically, coming back to our souls should not be done through a path of harmony, but in diversity, dis-order and justice' (Althaus-Reid, 2004e, p. 35). It is through our diverse loving experiences that we connect to God and build a just world.

The Queer Theologian and Her Community

The queer theologian fulfils a role of unmasking theology, by sharing her own contrasting experiences from the margins. 'Queer theologians by definition belong to the margins of society in more than one sense' (Althaus-Reid, 2008a, p. 105). First, simply by doing queer theology one is marginalized, outside the norm. The queer theologian discusses openly loving relationships in all their variety, unusual both in society and theology. For Althaus-Reid, 'Queer theologians are thus facilitators of the sexual traffic of the church's praxis' (Althaus-Reid, 2004e, p. 30). Queer theologians listen to and tell the real stories of love, even if the church doesn't want to hear them.

The queer theologian is clear about her own perspective, refusing to assume to speak for all. 'Queer theology is an "I" theology. The theologian doesn't hide in a grammatical essentialism, for instance, to use a "we" which presumes the authority of an academic body' (Isherwood and Althaus-Reid, 2004, p. 6). If I speak about my experience, I acknowledge it as valid but not universal. To be queer and to queer is to do a theology that remains in process.

We begin by telling our stories. Our sexual stories tell much more about how we relate to each other than just around sex. 'First, erotic stories are at the base of any human identity constructions' (Althaus-Reid, 2001b, p. 65). All our relationships include eros. These stories expand our understanding of life and love. 'Second, erotic stories are revelatory stories because they allow us to see something else, to reveal to us existence itself, especially in the elements of risk, the weighing of creative imagination in the process, and the envisaging of truth' (Althaus-Reid, 2001b, p. 65). In coming out with our stories, we share our realities and why the framework of the system needs to change; currently, frameworks and real life are mismatched and we are supposed to change to fit them. Instead, the frameworks need to change and expand to fit us.

Testimonies have always been part of the Christian tradition, though not usually sexual. We can read theology from these honest testimonies. 'The testimonio is an acknowledged narrative style that comes from voices at the margins and has been called a post-colonial intervention, outside the authorized theological discourses' (Althaus-Reid, 2008a, p. 113). We can understand the struggle in its diversity, listening to stories that destabilize our assumptions. When differences emerge, they run in parallel rather than try to resolve differences into a unified whole. 'As queer paradigms do not work by opposition but by differentiation, struggles are identified and multiply but not in an oppositional pattern' (Althaus-Reid, 2008a, p. 115). We can see the intersections of oppression and work to end them rather than prioritize one over another.

Unmasking and Expanding

In truth, Althaus-Reid articulated two concepts: queering theology and queer theologies. The term queer theology is a misnomer as one single theology should not emerge. 'Queer theology ... provides us with a flexible and plural framework of reflection ... to focus on mismatches and the ill-fitting life stories from those who are not part of centre-periphery thought. In queer thinking non-dualism means inclusivity and dialogue' (Althaus-Reid, 2001b, p. 63). Queering theology enables plurality. We find new theologies based on reality; these new theologies are not to be compromised to form one strand. The idea is not simply to destroy but to create alternatives. 'Like postmodernism, queer theology asks that we demystify, undo and subvert' (Isherwood and Althaus-Reid, 2004, p. 9). In a democratic discussion, we do not have a tyranny of the majority but a variety of voices heard and alternatives enabled to emerge. Queer theologies can enable us to build just communities.

Queering allows differences to emerge, in community and in theology. 'Queer theology is basically an example of high theological doubting or queering, irreverent in the sense that it tends to desacralize what has been made sacred for the sake of ideological interests' (Althaus-Reid, 2001b, p. 58). The beginning of queer theology is suspecting that theology is more complex than heterosexuality suggests. 'Queer theology (or theologies, to be more precise) is the complex result of a theological reflection that considers what the different constructions of sexuality and gender have to say of our understanding of God, love, and community' (Althaus-Reid, 2008c, p. 91). As noted in the previous chapter, heterosexuality itself is experientially diverse and enforcing a narrow frame of heterosexuality has caused oppression. While queering theology does not condemn heterosexuality, it critiques how the dominant framework excludes many heterosexual and non-heterosexual behaviours.

The goal is heterogeneity not homogeneity. Theologically, heterogeneity is important because the goal is not one theology but multiple diverse theologies in conversation. 'Queer theory becomes important as we consider theological issues of sexuality because, hermeneutically, theology needs to confront the irruption of the sexual subject in history' (Althaus-Reid, 2008c, p. 87). While traditional Christian theology prioritized heterosexuality in the context of marriage, queer theology considers other possibilities as ways of knowing God. Humans are sexually diverse and theology should reflect that.

The goal is to celebrate diversity, to care about difference, not to stop caring because there is difference. It is to shock us into seeing what we have never noticed before. Reading from reality rather than ideology exposes many assumptions. In sum, Althaus-Reid argued, 'And this is what a Queering process brings to theology: something that we could call a practice of Christian becoming which welcomes challenges and shifts in theology' (Althaus-Reid, 2006b, p. 250). Queering means celebrating the different ways to know God. 'If queer theology remains stubborn, not attempting to resolve the instability of both theology and feminism, the only "fixity" is the temporary, momentous revelations of new meaning' (Althaus-Reid,

2008a, p. 110). It is our open, honest conversation that is key. We want to open new avenues for theologizing, rather than create a closed systematic theology.

Queer theologies reject narrow definitions and expand the conversation. 'It is the theology that remembers the love that has been betrayed by dogmatic traditions and by the theological teaching of the church informed by ideologies of sexual exclusion' (Althaus-Reid, 2007c, p. 147). Queer theology begins with the marginalized and how they love. 'Queer theology is, then, a sexual theology with a difference: a passion for the marginalized' (Isherwood and Althaus-Reid, 2004, p. 6). Queer theology aims to help us move forward, engaging in the process of improvement and ending injustice. It centres on the excluded, starting with the last first. It works from the margins as they are.

This love-talk can help us to change the world. 'Queering theology provides us with more than a reflection: it is a Christian praxis which aims to rethink alternative and radical ways of transformation in our present world so shaken by the contradictions of globalization' (Isherwood and Althaus-Reid, 2004, p. 2). In this engagement with our loving relationships, we work towards justice. 'Let us never forget that lovemaking and working for justice go well together when we are engaged in the real struggle for the *alternative* project of the Kingdom of God, which is a transgressive and provocative project' (Althaus-Reid, 2001b, p. 67). Loving justly and working towards justice in all realms are important. We are not closing options but expanding and crafting alternatives. The church exiled loving relationships where God is also found. It is our diverse loving relationships with each other that can deepen our diverse loving relationships with God, and help us to build a more just world.

This perspective can also help us to understand the importance of developing loving relationships, so lacking in Western society with its capitalist and individualist foci.

Queer Theology can help to unmask much deeper mechanisms connecting the global expansion of capitalism and its brand theology with the critical exclusion of sainthood from the lives of the marginalized of the system ... It is that quality of difference in making the world holy by embracing elements of difference and understanding the oddity of Jesus as a Messiah against the normal or common sense, that makes Christian holiness a Queer holiness. (Althaus-Reid, 2003c, pp. 152–3)

Queer theology helps to show the connections between hierarchies in religion, our global economic systems and political systems, and how the definition of what is holy has been tainted by heterosexuality and patriarchy. Instead, holiness comes through loving each other and working towards justice, not fitting within a narrow heterosexual norm.

As we find these loving relationships, we begin to understand how theology has kept us from knowing God through its narrow framework. 'Queer theory also has implications for Christian ethics and practical theology, in questioning for instance the sexual economies of the Christian family and marriage' (Althaus-Reid, 2008c, p. 94). In this engagement with loving relationships, all our understandings of theological concepts will change and expand. 'If theology is a sexual act, to stand up for bigamy or polyamorous relationships is to stand also for a queering attitude to Christology, Mariology or the Trinity' (Althaus-Reid, 2004e, p. 27). All theological concepts have been framed in heterosexuality and patriarchy; all can be let out of their closets.

Reading the Bible Queerly

For many of us, our reading of the Bible is framed heterosexually; it is hard to unlearn this framing. The important piece of reading Scripture is to bring your true self into the room. To bring oneself into the discussion is to unmask and unpack what has been learned and read from one's own experience together with others. First, unlearn and see what might be in between the lines. 'There is a need to diagnose elements which stand in some form of opposition through the text to elements related to heterosexual thought ... Once these thoughts have been localized the relationships need to be inverted, dispersed and disrupted' (Althaus-Reid, 2003c, p. 80). Althaus-Reid suggested particularly examining examples of denigration because they clearly show hierarchies; for example, a text denigrating women shows the hierarchy of men over women (Althaus-Reid, 2003c, p. 80). When we see who is denigrated in the text, we can then see what diversity is condemned and who has been prioritized. What difference is disallowed? What framework limits the writing?

Reading from our own experience in community can help us see the text differently. My experience and reading may be different from yours.

> The experience of lesbians oppressed by gays, or bisexuals oppressed by almost everybody, may produce tensions and differences which are not reconcilable, which may need to stand side by side as simply different ... The attempt to situate our hermeneutical circle of interpretation around Queer solidarities, might allow us to ... foster the resistance ... to let go of patterns of subjugation of the Other. (Althaus-Reid, 2003c, p. 81)

As we see diverse readings, we learn to accept difference. The aim is not to all agree on one perspective but to see how we have denied the validity of experiences of others; it is to expand rather than limit interpretation.

The key is to read the Bible from the perspective of love. Who is loved? Who is excluded from love? 'Queering is also the art of deconstructing laws in search of justice, an art which comes from experiences of love at the margins of the lawful or, to use Christian terms, outside the redeemable' (Althaus-Reid, 2003c, pp. 78–9). Read the text to love others and do justice. Who do we need to learn to love?

Here, we can reread the story of Rahab, addressed in previous chapters. Althaus-Reid argued that 'Rahab is ... Wisdom standing alone against a process of making her straight: straight in the conversion towards a monotheistic culture and religion, manifested in a process of imperialist expansion'

(Althaus-Reid, 2007e, p. 132). Rahab can be read as representing Wisdom (female), forced to submit to the one male God. The biblical text sees Rahab's betrayal of her own people as a positive. However, we can also read it as a negative framing of difference. Althaus-Reid suggested that 'To read the Rahab narratives from this perspective is a permutative praxis, where we can recognize that real life experiences are sexually (ideologically) organized, and that includes those of the theologian herself' (Althaus-Reid, 2007e, p. 133). Underlying the Rahab text is a celebration of sameness and critique of difference, including sexuality. We need to recognize how we have been organized.

Queering God

Like theology, God needs to be let out of the closet. 'Queering theology is the path of God's own liberation ... The God who has come out, tired perhaps of being pushed to the edge by hegemonic sexual systems in theology, has made God's sanctuary on the Other side' (Althaus-Reid, 2003c, p. 4). Queer theology shows God outside heterosexuality. Our task is to find God among ourselves, among the margins. 'God is also queer, perhaps the first queer of all' (Althaus-Reid, 2004e, p. 28). We learn to know God through understanding our loving relationships. How might we come to know God through sex? Queering God means expanding understandings of God. The idea is to overcome the systematization and normalization of one concept of God.

In remembering the limitlessness of God several concepts emerge. First, God's relationships are unlimited; second, God is not static.

The first is the theological presentation of God as an immoderate, polyamorous God, whose self is composed in relation to multiple embraces and sexual indefinitions ... The second is the commitment of an omnisexual kenosis to destabilize sexual constructions of heterosexual readings of heterosexuality itself, bisexuality, gay and lesbian sexual identities and transvestite identities. (Althaus-Reid, 2003c, p. 57)

God is in deep relation as three, still becoming God. Understanding God as multiple as well as in multiple relationships can support our variety of relationships.

In these experiences, God is multiple, diverse, and these are positive qualities. 'Everything "bi", double, is seen in Christian heterosexual ethics as dubious, immoral' (Althaus-Reid, 2001b, p. 62). Our understanding of and relationship with God can be expanded through these inquiries, which accept multiplicity. 'A Queer proposal then is to modify God's master file with a new list of aberrancies (vagaries; things that go astray ...)' (Althaus-Reid, 2003c, p. 53). Queering is critical to overcome the dominant narrow framework and help us build relations with God.

In looking at God, we also need to consider the complexity of the Trinity. 'The task of Queer Theology is precisely to deepen this reflection on the sexual relationship manifested in the Trinity and to consider how God in the Trinity may come out in a relationship outside heterosexualism' (Althaus-Reid, 2003c, p. 46). The Trinity is a relationship of three. Althaus-Reid wanted to understand God through the notion of how we welcome the stranger, not the one like us but the different, how we come together in community.

Queering Jesus Christ

Queer theology begins, as indecent theology, with God becoming human in Jesus. There is much to God becoming Jesus that has not been explored, in particular the body of Jesus. As noted previously, Jesus comes into this world as a baby born and raised through childhood into adulthood (Isherwood and Althaus-Reid, 2004, p. 7). Jesus' body, fully human, and other bodies can help us to know God. The divine experienced being fully human.

Althaus-Reid built on the work of Goss here. The first premise is to read Christ to reveal God. The second is to remember that we are not trying to find one framework but a process involving many avenues; Scriptures are open, not closed. Third, we need to consider Jesus' sexuality, and, fourth, we need to see Jesus in the marginalized. 'Unless we can locate Jesus' passion in the real life of people we will not be able to understand the meaning of incarnation nor the subversion of bodies that resurrection implies' (Althaus-Reid, 2004b, p. 169). In Jesus' case, the body survived even death. Althaus-Reid articulated that Jesus was queer, outside the norm, dying and being resurrected many times (Althaus-Reid, 2004b, pp. 175–6). Althaus-Reid wondered if the killing of Jesus was an attempt to settle Jesus down, with one ending. Yet, Jesus is divine and so this is impossible.

Queering theology, for Althaus-Reid, meant unpacking the harms of heterosexual theology and searching for God in those places and behaviours excluded by such theology. God is much too expansive to be kept in a closet. Human beings too, with our diverse ways of loving, need to be freed from our own closets to know God.

Suggested reading

Althaus-Reid, M., 2001b, 'Outing Theology: Thinking Christianity out of the Church Closet', *Feminist Theology*, 27, pp. 57–67.

Althaus-Reid, M., 2003c, 'Introduction', in *The Queer God*, pp. 1–4, New York: Routledge.

Althaus-Reid, M., 2004e, 'Queer I Stand: Lifting the Skirts of God', in Althaus-Reid, M. and L. Isherwood, eds, *The Sexual Theologian: Essays on Sex, God, and Politics*, pp. 99–109, London: T&T Clark International.

Althaus-Reid, M., 2008c, 'On Queer Theory and Liberation Theology: The Irruption of the Sexual Subject in Theology', in Althaus-Reid, M., ed., *Homosexualities*, pp. 83–96, London: SCM Press.

Note

1 Judith Butler (1956–) is a US feminist philosopher and critical theorist.

12

A Marginal God

For Althaus-Reid, God is not a god of the centre who visits the margins. Rather, God emerges from and lives in the margins. God is a marginal God. The supposed God of the centre is a god created and fixed in order to support heterosexuality and capitalism. This frame is too narrow to contain God. The God of the margins is the God found at the leading edges. The edges guide us forward towards a fuller understanding of God. Key for Marcella was that the excluded are the leading edge of a God becoming more fully God.

God: Imprisoned by and Exiled from the Centre

Althaus-Reid argued that the centre imprisoned and then exiled God through its narrow dominant frameworks. 'God Godself had disappeared in some concentration camp but the Church had not realized it as yet' (Althaus-Reid, 2006b, p. 256). The dominant form of Christianity forced God into a small box. God, being far more expansive, went into exile, where God could be free to be Godself.

God exiled Godself from traditional theology because of its insistence on patriarchy, heterosexuality and domination. 'For the Queer God is the God who went into exile with God's people and remained there in exile with them' (Althaus-Reid, 2004b, p. 146). As God's people, the excluded provide God with a home to be Godself when the 'centre' does not. God is free to become fully God at the margins. Our understanding of God should change as we live and work with those at the margins.

Liberation theology did begin to consider God at the margins but at first this God was seen to have similar characteristics to the God of the centre, just in a different location.

> We may say that the path from the marginalization of God to the God at the margins lies in the fact that we may become tougher, without losing our tenderness. Liberation theology was ... able to find God at the margins. The tough part was the questioning and the suspicion, which worked by not giving God an authority at the centre. (Althaus-Reid, 2001a, pp. 29–30)

Liberation theologians moved to the margins to see God there, rather than remain at the centre. Liberation theology understood that God does not belong to the centre; God cannot not be narrowly defined or constricted. God is an expansive, loving God. However, liberation theology has not yet fully seen how God at the margins is different.

Examining the margins shows us that God was squeezed out from the centre's narrowly defined image of God. At the margins, we have a better chance to learn how God actively lives and works with the excluded, expanding and becoming more of Godself.

> Popular theology comes from people who need the emotional strength ... to live the extra twenty-four hours of their lives which start without much hope of finding food ... The two basic assumptions of the readings are that God is an ally, and that faith has agency to change circumstances. (Althaus-Reid, 2001a, pp. 28–9)

For the excluded, God is on their side, actively working with them in the struggle to survive. They live with God, rather than define God. This God is very different from the God of the centre.

A Marginal God

For Althaus-Reid, we need to begin to know God as God is, rather than keep any of our previous assumptions. 'That may be God the stranger amongst us, a queer God of the margins. This is an important point, with consequences, namely the location of God (and Christ Jesus) in the margins' (Althaus-Reid, 2006b, p. 258). God, imprisoned by the powerful, has been rescued by the powerless. Our recognition that God lives at the margins should overturn much of our traditional theology. 'That critical location of God in our communities and in theology is a Queer one, and constitutes a process of sexual decolonization of our Christian discourses' (Althaus-Reid, 2006b, p. 258). Queering God requires queering God's location and our framing of God. God is free to be God without our attempt to systemize and constrain.

Althaus-Reid moved beyond articulating that God moved from the centre to the margins and stated that God lives with and becomes fully God at the margins. We need to see this God at the margins for who God is, and become comfortable with God at the margins rather than try to re-centre this God. Early liberationists still worked in a 'centring' mode. God is at the margins because God has chosen to live at the margins and emerges in relationships at the margins; this God is not the god of the centre. 'What informs this caminata is the desire not to make of God an occasional and compassionate visitor to the margins of the margins but to rediscover that God is a truly marginal God' (Althaus-Reid, 2004b, p. 146). Will we also move to the margins to experience God? Or will we keep trying to bring God back to a centre with just a few more characteristics?

Unfortunately, we have the urge to build a framework for God with certain characteristics and we 'include' everything we see into our preconceived framework. 'In many instances, in a cruel twist of power, the so-called theologies from the margins have been manipulated to support or justify the ideologies of the centre by simply restoring given understandings in an exercise of cultural translations' (Althaus-Reid, 2004c, p. 369). We have to resist the centre, resisting dualisms, resisting any final or set definitions. 'In theology, the paradox is that the margins need to depart from the margins of a theology based on dualist obsessions' (Althaus-Reid, 2001b, p. 63). The margins need to move forward, not look back towards a centre. We need to shift our mapping.

The God of the centre is in fact a false god, created by the centre for its own uses. Instead, God is a marginal God. 'The serious engagement of theology with people's struggles required another movement, this time from a God at the margins (still partaking of central definitions) to a more radical "marginal God"' (Althaus-Reid, 2001a, p. 30). If we only see God as moving from the centre to the margins, God remains the same God but in a different location, and that location has been defined by the centre itself as marginal. 'We need to concede that God at the margins is a theologically geographical concept, and as such part of a master's map' (Althaus-Reid, 2001a, p. 31). People at the margins have their own maps, unrelated to the centre. There, God is present, living and struggling with them. God becomes Godself at the margins, unrelated to the centre.

Theology too changes when God emerges from the margins. 'It is the marginal God's project which can lead us outside the developmental model in theology ... Margins are not margins but geographies in their own right' (Althaus-Reid, 2001a, p. 32). Development tends to consider a line of progress towards the success measured by the centre, but places can be considered in and of themselves. The marginal God need not be compared to the centre. Instead of wondering what nuances we can add to traditional theologies, theologizing from the margins upends and expands theology. It is not the margins versus the centre but an expanding and flowing of Godself.

We can learn to see God in the margins as God truly is. 'It is at the margins that God is found as the material excess of innocent suffering ... It is God touching God's own limits in the untouchables from Buenos Aires' (Althaus-Reid, 2004a, p. 394). God expands beyond God's limits at the margins, becoming a larger God. 'It is even wiser ... to make people at the margins the people of God, those who are at the leading edge and not simply those who are at the receiving end of a central institution' (Althaus-Reid, 2003c, p. 162). We need to see the margins as the leading edges of God. The margins pull us away from a falsely centred God towards an emerging God. This God is in movement, expanding and loving.

God changes and grows when emerging from the margins. At the margins, people look for places God has hidden in order to expand their understanding of God. 'There are unauthorized sites of divinity ... in which fears of unfaithfulness in theological reflections and hopes for transformation keep bad company ... untouched, seldom-addressed painful margins in the life of every Christian, which only a marginal God can address' (Althaus-Reid, 2001a, p. 31). God has remained hidden in our margins, hidden in the places we want to ignore; will we recognize and see this God? All those places that traditional Christianity has excluded or disparaged, God is there.

God lives with and within the excluded, becoming fully God. If our theology does not emerge from the excluded, we miss seeing God. 'When we say that the excluded represent the excess of the excess, we refer to the excess of degradation to which human lives can be subjected; the excess of anonymity and invisibility, too ... locus of the excess of God' (Althaus-Reid, 1998a, 253–4). In the extreme harshness of life in the communities of the excluded, we find a new God. The excluded are crafted in the image of God and show us more faces of God.

Examining notions like Madame Edwarda, God the prostitute, can help us understand a broader, more diverse God. 'She [Madame Edwarda] is not only a woman-God at the Margin, but a Marginal woman-God' (Althaus-Reid, 2000b, p. 212). As of yet, there are not many written examples of a marginal God, but we do have many stories and experiences, if only we will listen to them. Where else can we see a marginalized God? God the old woman, God the street child, God the 'madman' in the asylum.

God emerges from the experiences of those our society deems 'mad'; those society rejects are the face of God. The homeless person we walk by in the street is the face of God; the community living under the bridge is the face of God.

> El tocado (the touched one) conveys the meaning of several epistemological irregularities: tocado refers to someone outside the logic of a system; a slightly mad person ... It is as if in el tocado we are told of a God who disrupts the orders of representing or greeting (touching) the divine. (Althaus-Reid, 2004a, p. 400)

Madness, by definition, is behaviour outside our normative psychology. God too may be mad, outside our psychological parameters. Those who are completely excluded from our normative systems can help us to know God, the parts of God we have avoided and rejected.

God at the margins shows us our fear of really understanding God. This fear of really understanding God has influenced traditional theology, which has not fully examined the implications of God becoming human in Jesus, as the body chapter argued. God expanded and changed when God became Jesus; God was somehow dissatisfied with the way things were.

> God in Christ was a God with an identity crisis .... a God putting Godself under judgement, a self-judgement involving a type of quest identity for Jesus, was at the same time a becoming messiah and an unfinished God ... The queer man of God came out and ... conquered hearts and his community was becoming strong enough to present a different or alternative lifestyle ... The whole cycle of public humiliation ... ends with this poor, fragile young God dying a miserable death. (Althaus-Reid, 2004b, pp. 173–4)

God may have solved God's own crisis by becoming Jesus, becoming human. That Jesus was rejected by society, crucified. However, God's becoming and changing did not end with Jesus, it continues today. Society rejected God's coming out as Jesus, during his lifetime. We again have the choice to let God come out or to reject God. God is still becoming God today.

God became Jesus, coming out of Godself, emerging and expanding, experiencing life as a full human being. 'Reading the ambiguous text of Jesus, we read the text of a God who does not fit Godself anymore and needs to come out of some divine closet as an immigrant God or a drag God trespassing the law' (Althaus-Reid, 2004a, p. 401). God came out as Jesus, transgressing many norms, including the concept of God as solely spirit. We can begin to envision such a God from the perspective of those excluded, rejected by society.

> El Tocado represents ... a God whose knowledge invites us also to undress the discipline and pedagogy of sexual, gender, and political assumptions about God ... Between the cartoneros, the 'card-collectors' ... and Jesus as el Tocado, we are in the presence of two mutual exclusions of the law of tact: the untouchable people of the global expansion of Capitalism and el Tocado as a different, marginal way of a divine economic and affective production. (Althaus-Reid, 2004a, pp. 401–3)

The 'touched' one is normally one who we do not want to touch. In the same way, for those with privilege, the marginal God seems untouchable. We have to touch this God. We find God and love among the untouchables. 'God can only be touched in the revelation of the untouchables, the ones whose lives are prophetic because they denounce with their presence in the cities the injustice of the present economic and sexual systems' (Althaus-Reid, 2004a, p. 403). In fact, it is in touching the mad God that we find God. God can only be let out of the closet by those also outside the closet. So, too, our notion of Jesus needs to be freed. Traditional Christianity has also imprisoned Jesus.

Theology from the margins is neither attached to nor intimidated by systematic theologies. The excluded do not need to read all the fathers of the church before meeting God. A theology from the margins lives with God. As Althaus-Reid argued, 'Sometime theology should declare an independence day, and start anew, from the real grassroots of marginal communities to find a God who is less domesticated, and less brainwashed' (Althaus-Reid, 2001a, p. 32). God is in mutual relationship with those at the margins, not requiring submission or academic scholarship. Seeing this God could upend our notions of sin, salvation, heaven, hell and so forth. For example, the margins do not relate to God in a king/servant model.

> Mutual dependency in relation to God may then supersede the monarchic conceptualization of the God-King ... solidarity amongst equals is more important in communities of resistance than hierarchical dreams ... it will take a marginal God to show us that the best of our history of solidarity and strategical organization for change comes not from ... central constructions. (Althaus-Reid, 2001a, p. 33)

The marginal God rejects hierarchy in favour of solidarity; perhaps we could reconsider what a new heaven and new earth would be like beyond the 'kingdom' model. God does not arrive at the margins from the centre with theology in tow, with all the answers. God lives and works with the margins in community, learning and becoming in relation with others.

Theologies from the excluded show us what we have not seen about God, for example, an expanded notion of communion. 'If we are part of a Church which has taken a preferential option for the excluded, we need to think about doing theology from what can be called "the archives from hell"' (Althaus-Reid, 2005a, p. 103). Theology from these archives is theology from the everyday lives of the excluded, on garbage dumps, in insane asylums, under bridges. These locations emerge 'as a Eucharistic gathering, for it shows the presence of God manifested in people's praxis of solidarity ... while encouraging us towards a praxis of love and justice inspired by the project of the Kingdom of God' (Althaus-Reid, 2005a, p. 104). Solidarity and communion with each other and God at the harshest points of life are key. Communion becomes scavenging for food in a garbage dump. While much Christian theology ignores the excluded for their varied transgressions of formal morality, in fact God is there; we need to see God there and understand God there. 'The theology of the excluded is always concrete and transcendence comes from an understanding of the "ordinary" in God who takes side with the excluded, even if they are wearing high heels and make-up when searching for refuse material' (Althaus-Reid, 2005a, p. 107). God and theology are constantly becoming in communities of the excluded; this God does not look at decent dress codes or behaviour, but simply lives with the excluded.

In sum, Althaus-Reid argued, 'Christianity is a religion built around a destitute God who came for destitute people' (Althaus-Reid, 2006d, p. 118). Let's return to an expansive notion of God, not the God in a box at the centre. The excluded with their post-colonial perspective can upend theology. It is not a focus on life and hope that is necessary but reflection on the realities of the excluded. God can be found among the marginalized, where God is free to be Godself. 'In every community of excluded people and in every inch of the struggle for sexual and economic justice, the queer God manifests Godself with full glory, power and grace' (Althaus-Reid, 2004b, p. 176). When we limit God to the centre among people of privilege, we miss out on a deeper understanding of God.

Suggested reading

Althaus-Reid, M., 2001a, 'The Divine Exodus of God: Involuntary Marginalized, Taking an Option for the Margins, or Truly Marginal?' in Jeanrond, W. G. and C. Theobald, eds, *God, Experience and Mystery*, pp. 27–33, London: SCM Press.

Althaus-Reid, M., 2004a, 'El Tocado (Le Toucher): Sexual Irregularities in the Translation of God (The Word) in Jesus', in Sherwood, Y. and K. Hart, eds, *Derrida and Religion: Other Testaments*, pp. 393–405, New York: Routledge.

Althaus-Reid, M., 2006b, 'Graffiti on the Walls of the Cathedral of Buenos Aires: Doing Theology, Love and Politics at the Margins', in Hoelzl, M. and G. Ward, eds, *Religion and Political Thought*, London: Continuum.

13

Crucifixions/Resurrections

Throughout her work, Marcella provided everyday examples of crucifixions and resurrections to examine the concept of God. If God is emerging from the margins, then what might crucifixions and resurrections at the margins look like? What might they tell us about God and our systems?

For Althaus-Reid, we have lost a focus on the horror of death and the importance of resurrections in traditional theologies. 'Death (as deadly structures amongst us, such as imperial and neo-liberal policies) needs to become again a frontier or we shall lose the power to act ... Without death as a frontier we are in the domain of absolutes' (Althaus-Reid, 2006c, p. 42). Our structures of death can be overcome. Death is important because it shows us not an ending but a possibility for resurrection.

Jesus' Crucifixions/Resurrections

The first narrative of crucifixion and resurrection is the story of Jesus. Althaus-Reid argued that even this event was a community narrative. Jesus did not die and resurrect alone. 'With Jesus' resurrection, a whole community of people who suffered his loss when he was crucified came back to life ... Death took on another meaning; the resurrection became the paradigm showing us the durability and indestructibility of life and justice' (Althaus-Reid, 2004b, p. 113). In a sense, when Jesus died, the community died, and when Jesus was resurrected so too was his community. The community realized death was not the end. However, for Althaus-Reid, Jesus went through several deaths and rebirths throughout his time on earth.

Understanding Jesus' life as a series of deaths and resurrections opens the story. It is also important to note that not all of the Gospels focus on the final resurrection; the early version of Mark ended with Jesus' death. However, there is a broader story of crucifixions throughout Jesus' life, along with the final crucifixion.

> In a way, he lost his family and social location. Second, he suffers from economic death ... a poor man, rendered invisible by the economic power of his time, a nobody. And finally, torture and death by crucifixion ends his messianic mission ... He becomes an unemployed God, a devalued, misunderstood God outside the market. In everything Jesus did, God's abundant presence was there, but nevertheless, for society, he was a failure. (Althaus-Reid, 2004b, p. 169)

Jesus died from his family, died from economic life, and was rejected by political and religious society. Jesus the messiah was crucified but Jesus the messiah was also resurrected. Society killed Jesus but that was not the end.

For Althaus-Reid, the final crucifixion attempted to end the destabilizing force that was Jesus. 'The cross is the attempt to kill once and for all the multiple resurrections of a Queer Jesus, to fix him once and for ever ... that no Queer God would ... exceed the border limits of a fatigued heterosexual foundational epistemology' (Althaus-Reid, 2004b, p. 176). Our theology threatens to do what the crucifixion tried to do, to fix Jesus and God in one location, as static and stable, ending with death rather than life. However, the cycle of life and death continues and God and Jesus continue to be and to become.

She also highlighted the aspects of the story that society would have considered daft, made fun of, just as the deaths of many of the marginalized are seen as trivial and mildly amusing.

> In the taking of Jesus the scene is not without comic elements. First there is the description of the company of soldiers creeping up the slope with a variety of swords and weapons to deal with a handful of men who apparently cannot keep their

eyes open ... And then there is the incident of the young man who, curiously, was wearing nothing but a piece of linen cloth. As the soldiers attempt to apprehend him he dashed off naked like a streaker, leaving the soldiers holding the sheet. (Althaus-Reid, 2004b, pp. 174–5)

The ridiculousness of the soldiers' actions can make Jesus' situation seem silly, as if he could have avoided it, but it can also show the ridiculousness of killing Jesus. The seriousness of death and resurrection also has a comic or ironic element, leading us to question why crucifixions happen and why resurrections then need to occur. Yes, deaths can bring about rebirths, but maybe these deaths need not occur in the first place.

In fact, our theology doesn't often deal with the horror of crucifixion in any more depth than death. The horrific crucifying of Jesus seems to be forgotten in the discussion of the resurrection. 'Beyond the complex debate on the dynamics of the voluntary and the involuntary in the crucifixion of Christ ... there is more to crucifixion than mere death ... Our understanding of life ... is ... dependent on a hermeneutics of crucifixion' (Althaus-Reid, 2006c, p. 37). The theology that argues Jesus' death simply led to resurrection tames the horror of the powerful's rejection of Jesus. Death was horrific and unwanted but overcome by rebirth.

Althaus-Reid argued that we also miss the love for life in our understanding of the crucifixion and resurrection. Althaus-Reid articulated Christ's resurrection as a coming out, a rejection of death because he loved life so much.

> This Christ gives us food for thought if we consider resurrection as a coming out experience ... A person comes out ... because that person loves life so much that she has decided to come out from structures of death and oppression ... Christ's resurrected presence can only be seen then as a craving, an enthusiastic passion for life and justice. (Althaus-Reid, 2000c, p. 123)

People come out because they no longer respect death and deadly structures, just as Jesus did. Instead, we can resurrect alternatives to our death-seeking structures. We need resurrections in our communities today too, overcoming our crucifixions.

The life, death and resurrection of Jesus signalled something new, not a reform. Crucifixions today also call for something new. 'A new order of things ... was desired by the Messianic community who accompanied [Jesus] until his end ... Christology needs to queer the basic tenets of our Christian experience, and that includes the politics of crucifixions' (Althaus-Reid, 2007d, p. 291). Jesus' followers wanted a new society. As with Jesus' death and resurrection, our deaths today cry out for building something new, not recreating the old.

Everyday Crucifixions/Resurrections

For Althaus-Reid, Jesus needs to be situated among his community and among our own communities of the excluded today to understand what crucifixions and resurrections mean. Just as Jesus' story contained multiple crucifixions and resurrections, so too do our stories. Althaus-Reid encouraged us to explore everyday crucifixions and resurrections.

One of the theological resurrections Althaus-Reid noted was the appearance of women's bodies in theology, from her work and the work of others like Isherwood. 'The bodies of women, and specifically of marginalized women in church and society, have reappeared in theological discourse to produce a crisis, a crisis in the sense of God's judgment upon the patriarchal ideologies' (Althaus-Reid, 2011, p. 443). The resurrection of women in theology has challenged hierarchical patriarchal theology. Women's bodies challenge theology; will we enable the excluded to resurrect too?

Althaus-Reid argued the system crucifies the excluded today as well; the excluded need resurrection. 'The amount of people sacrificed by the Global Capitalist system is of such magnitude in terms of suffering and numbers that it can only be compared to the suffering of a tortured god dying on a cross' (Althaus-Reid, 2007d, pp. 294–5). God lives and suffers alongside us; God is killed and excluded in many ways, just as we are. We continue to crucify Christ as we crucify others. Althaus-Reid told of the death of a boy in Latin America, comparing it to Christ's crucifixion, as described in Chapter 8. Monito Galvan was tortured to death and 'crowned' by putting a plastic bag over his head, representing his glue-sniffing habit. Althaus-Reid argued that this crucifixion was more realistic than Jesus', since we gloss over the horror of the crucifixion (Althaus-Reid, 2003c, p. 150). Like Christ, Galvan was crowned a king, mocked and murdered. We have lost this meaning in Christianity. Jesus did not want to die; the crucifixion was a horrific event.

For Althaus-Reid, it is the job of Christians, queer theologians in particular, to resurrect the different. She offered a story of a murdered transvestite in Argentina:

> a story of love, poverty and hope of resurrections ... a body being found on the road ... An indecent transvestite lay there ... they represent something liminal which has crossed borders and has dislocated the almost spatial ideology of heterosexuality ... The preoccupation is what to do with the body. The body should disappear ... They have killed a faggot, but she will come back. Cruci/fictions: messianic deaths. (Althaus-Reid, 2004b, pp. 167–8)

A transwoman was killed for being different and all society wants is for her to disappear. We have seen the crucifixion, now will we support the resurrection? Can we see Jesus as a crucified transvestite? Why do our systems crucify the different? 'In Argentina, transvestites are at a crossroads of public worship and church and state tactics of extermination ... Jesus in drag, dressed in a royal purple cloak with a crown of thorns. He is the subject of laughter ... just as the transvestite' (Althaus-Reid, 2004b, p. 168). Christ was dressed up and mocked before death, as we mock and kill the excluded today. Jesus was outside the system as transpeople are today.

In the same way that we need to ask why society crucified Jesus, we can ask why society continues to crucify others. We can also ask why we allow this killing to continue.

The killings of homosexuals in Argentinian society have within them a necessity of biblical proportions, manifesting the purifying rituals of the different in society. In the tabloids, the killing of queers is a genre in itself, desired to produce a mixture of moralization and amusement in the readers. (Althaus-Reid, 2004b, p. 174)

Political and religious society saw Jesus as a threat, as society sees homosexuality and transgenderism today. The media portrays the marginalized who are killed as asking for death, as Jesus' crucifixion is sometimes interpreted as crucial to restore humanity's relationship with God, as if Jesus wanted to die. However, Jesus overcame death, restoring life.

Althaus-Reid noted that many in Latin America suffered crucifixions during dictatorships and still wait for resurrections today. 'The women of El Salvador exemplify what it means for Christian people to be the witnesses of the cross and the resurrection ... This is a Theology of Memory, counting crosses and resurrections, and it is being developed by poor women in Latin America' (Althaus-Reid, 2004b, p. 114). Theology's role is to remember the unjust deaths, naming them and condemning them. Unjust deaths require resurrections to work towards justice, even if the resurrection is simply acknowledging that a death occurred, that the government did torture and kill. Justice requires an acknowledgement of and an end to injustice.

In part, this resurrection is simply to remember the dead through telling stories, so people can work towards restorative justice. Women are the key story-bearers. 'Fleeing from the massacres through the mountains, and experiencing all sorts of suffering related to their attempt to escape their pursuers ... This was called *la guinda*, and became a theological focus for a reflection on death and resurrection' (Althaus-Reid, 2004b, p. 118). Women escaped to the mountains to avoid being killed. Women relive this exodus story and the loss of the many killed through their worship today. Our re-creation and commemoration of losses is a form of resurrection.

The narratives of crucifixion and resurrection appeared throughout Latin America during these dictatorial regimes, comparing the killing of dissidents to the killing of Jesus, hoping for similar resurrections, not of the individuals but of the possibility of life for the oppressed.

> In Nicaragua, peasant paintings depicted the open tombs and the resurrections of Che Guevara and the Sandinistas killed during the revolution, coming to life again together with Jesus ... the resurrection *de abajo,* of the people who are oppressed and die different sort of deaths every day. (Althaus-Reid, 2000c, pp. 121–2)

The marginalized imagine all their dead resurrected with Jesus. The struggle towards justice is a struggle of people to overcome death, to be able to live. Death is ever present and for many of the excluded awakening in the morning is a resurrection, reborn for another day.

We see crucifixions every day in the news and fail to recognize them as such. We also fail to see that resurrections need to follow.

> A scene from ... the life, crucifixion, and resurrection of people and their ideas of economic justice and peace in the midst of the current chaotic crisis of the expansion of capitalism ... What was the crucifixion of a man, he argued, when whole communities can no longer afford the minimum required for a life with dignity? ... The newspaper article ... comes from the Paraguay of two years ago, when a group of people protested against job losses and the State's disregard for the life of the patients in a local hospital trapped by poverty. (Althaus-Reid, 2006c, pp. 35–6)

Similar to Jesus' crucifixion, Althaus-Reid narrated the story of another crucifixion in Paraguay. While the news highlighted a person who voluntarily crucified themselves in protest, the media ignored the evidence of everyday crucifixions, which spawned the need to protest. We fail to recognize everyday crucifixions of humans, allowing, enabling and supporting these deaths. Only a voluntary crucifixion brought attention to the expanding harm.

In fact, voluntary crucifixions as a form of protest have emerged across Latin America, bringing to light the horror of people killed by poverty and marginalization every day. 'Crucifixions are back ... As the blood of the just, clamouring to God, becomes a tangible reality, the idea of crucifixion loosed from piety suddenly appears; a dark symbol and certainly not for faint-hearted Christians' (Althaus-Reid, 2006c, p. 36). Indigenous and other excluded people re-enact the horror of crucifixion to show daily horrors. The aim is to highlight the crucifying of people every day, ignored and excluded by society. Just as society killed Jesus, so too society kills people daily. We need to understand the horrors occurring daily. This recognition will only occur when we remember the horror of Jesus' death.

> There have been scenes in public parks, where groups of people literally queued at lunch time to be participants in 'mock crucifixions' ... Wooden crosses expressed the reality of authentic crucifixions in the life of ordinary people suffering under ... the disregard for human life. (Althaus-Reid, 2007d, pp. 291–2)

These crucifixions represent the harm our capitalist economic system causes. Death enables resurrection, to experience life anew. Will we allow God, Jesus and varied understandings of the divine to resurrect? To enable people to live?

Canaan is rarely thought of from the perspective of needing resurrection, but many people and places have experienced crucifixion and await resurrection. How much have we lost in our theologizing that used one dominant group or narrative to oppress another? These new crucifixions offer us a new way to think about resurrections, not as bringing back one true theology but as letting those understandings of God that we have killed, rise again. God is in community with the excluded experiencing their daily crucifixion with them. Will we enable ourselves to see God?

Althaus-Reid argued that Latin Americans think more in terms of Canaan than the exodus story, which became a focus in early liberation theology. As with Canaan, Althaus-Reid argues that Latin America was crucified. Can it resurrect? 'Crucifixion could be inter-textually read as the original existential experience of the continent: that is, the sense of the sacred perished or at least was heavily devalued and demonized for centuries to come' (Althaus-Reid, 2006c, p. 39). Althaus-Reid explained how some of the indigenous people spend the entire month of Easter beside a cross in a park. Latin Americans deeply connect with the experience of crucifixion; their cultures and histories were crucified.

> If the Original Nations read the events of Passion Week from the perspective of their own experience of crucifixions it is because Latin America is in many ways Canaan ... The crucifixions of the excluded ... confront us as one of the most powerful ghosts of Christian faith: the crucified Canaanites. (Althaus-Reid, 2006c, p. 40)

The indigenous see themselves as Canaan, still needing to be resurrected. Christianity needs to contend with the crucifixions it has supported and crafted. It needs to enable and support resurrections, rather than continue its harm.

Can we reclaim our memories and our own realities? The indigenous see themselves in the crucified Jesus. Can we see that we have crucified difference? Will we listen? 'The cross ... becomes a form of communication ... Popular crucifixions as protest inauguration seem to violate something pre-established in the linguistic community of the Church, a community used to a sense of the proper use of authority based on logocentrism' (Althaus-Reid, 2006c, p. 41). Crucifixions become a way of dialoguing with dominant society. Can voluntary crucifixions disrupt this dominant framework? Can we begin a dialogue that prioritizes the excluded?

Althaus-Reid argued that we need to see and deal with everyday crucifixions and find out how to resurrect. 'If crucifixions regain their novelty and transgression, then the resurrection will have the possibility of announcing new life' (Althaus-Reid, 2006c, p. 38). Rather than see Jesus' crucifixion as mundane, we need to remember how shocking it was. When we are shocked by a voluntary crucifixion, Althaus-Reid stated, it shows us that we have failed to remember the meaning of the cross. 'There is a hermeneutical function in the popular crucifixions of the excluded and marginalized in Latin America, which help us not just to reread the event of Christ's death and resurrection but to reorganize a tentative hermeneutics of liberation' (Althaus-Reid, 2006c, p. 38). Voluntary crucifixions help us take seriously Christ's life and death and lives and deaths today. Many people are brutally killed and in need of resurrection. Theologies fail to see the need for everyday resurrections, even liberation theologies. Yet those at the margins rely on God for exactly that, hence the need to recognize a marginal God. Expanding our understanding of crucifixion and resurrection will help to expand our ways of relating to God, not as submission but in mutual relationship, suffering together and maybe even thriving together.

How are we still crucifying God? Will we allow God to resurrect, to become God anew, outside our narrow framework? This freeing of God and of ourselves was Althaus-Reid's hope.

Suggested reading

Althaus-Reid, M., 2004b, 'Doing the Theology of Memory: Counting Crosses and Resurrections', in *From Feminist Theology to Indecent Theology*, ch. 8, pp. 113–23, London: SCM Press.

Althaus-Reid, M., 2004b, 'Scenes from Queer Cruci/Fictions: *Matan a una Marica* ('They Killed a Faggot')', in *From Feminist Theology to Indecent Theology*, ch. 12, pp. 166–76, London: SCM Press.

Althaus-Reid, M., 2006c, 'On Dying Hard: Lessons from Popular Crucifixions and Undisciplined Resurrections in Latin America', in Queiruga, A. T., L. C. Susin and J. Sobrino, eds, *The Resurrection of the Dead*, pp. 35–43, London: SCM Press.

Conclusion

Althaus-Reid wanted us to upend our ideas of what is normal, by focusing on real experiences. The crucifixions and resurrections we see across the globe today can help us begin this process. We can rethink our understandings of the life, death and resurrection of Christ. The God of the margins also expands our notions, urging us to see God in places we normally avoid. So too, Althaus-Reid urges us to queer all our theological constructions from our realities and the realities of the excluded. In particular, we need to reject the narrow dominant framework of heterosexuality, which has harmed and excluded many. Thinking of indecent alternatives as a positive can destabilize our 'normative' theologies. Our alternatives should emerge from our bodies, as they are and as they experience life. Women's bodies in particular can help us find God and the sacred beyond the male heterosexual framework. The realities of our bodily experiences, alongside the experiences of the excluded, can help us to unmask the harms of capitalism and form alternatives. A post-colonial analysis is key here to unpack what European systems have deemed normative. In this way, liberation theologies and feminist theologies can be truly liberative. Following the hermeneutical circle of action and reflection enables us to better know God in community.

Moving forward, we can consider crafting theologies from particularly denigrated female body parts. We can also work with emerging changes in society. For example, the concepts of sex and sexuality have become more fluid among our young adults, as has transitioning. What would fluidity rather than any chosen sex or gender location do to our theory and theology? Finally, there are emerging economic alternatives to consider, even among European and US economists. Much has changed since Althaus-Reid's death in 2009. While her theological analysis remains prophetic and still far beyond many of our frames, we can work with and push forward many alternatives.

In sum, Althaus-Reid wanted to help us free ourselves from dominating constructs that keep us from knowing God. For Althaus-Reid, theologies are so mired in particular dominant frameworks that theology alienates us from God rather than connects us to God. Theologies exile God because God is too expansive to be imprisoned in the centre. We fail to prioritize the excluded, with whom God lives and works. We fail to see how we crucify others as Christ was crucified. And we fail to see the need for resurrections. We need to subject all we have learned to suspicion, trying to see our realities. For Althaus-Reid, the goal is not to formulate one theology but to celebrate the diverse ways of knowing God. In so doing, we would learn to love and to work towards justice. I urge you to read Marcella's work and take on the task of freeing God and queering theology.

> May we together, by the grace of God, stand always *queer* with love, courage and a passion for justice. (Althaus-Reid, 2004e, p. 37)

Bibliography

Althaus-Reid, M., 1993, 'Paul Ricoeur and the Methodology of the Theology of Liberation: The Hermeneutics of J. Severino Croatto, Juan Luis Segundo and Clodovis Boff', University of St Andrews.

Althaus-Reid, M., 1995, 'Exceeding the Written Testimony: Towards a "Non-recorded" Renewal of Theology, Ministry and God's People', in Pobee, J. S., ed., *Theology, Ministry and Renewal of God's People: Sixteen Bible Studies*, pp. 10 –19, Geneva: World Council of Churches.

Althaus-Reid, M., 1996a, 'Both Indecent and Ex-centric: Teaching Feminist Theology for Articulation or for Exoticism?', in Althaus-Reid, M., ed., *Liberating the Vision: Papers of the Summer School, 24–28 May*, pp. 71–7, Southampton: Centre for Contemporary Theology, LSU.

Althaus-Reid, M., 1996b, 'The Indecency of Her Teaching: Notes for Cuceb Teaching of Feminist Theology in Europe', in Fiorenza, E. S. and M. S. Copeland, eds., *Feminist Theology in Different Contexts*, pp. 133–40, London: SCM Press.

Althaus-Reid, M., 1996c, 'Liberation Theology', in Fahlbusch, E., J. Lochman, J. S. Mbiti, J. Pelikan and L. Vischer, eds, *Encyclopedia of Christianity*, pp. 387–90, Leiden: Brill.

Althaus-Reid, M., 1997, 'Sexual Strategies in Practical Theology: Indecent Theology and the Plotting of Desire with Some Degree of Success', *Theology and Sexuality*, 7, pp. 45–52.

Althaus-Reid, M., 1998a, 'The Hermeneutics of Transgression', in Schrijver, G. D., ed., *Liberation Theologies on Shifting Grounds: A Clash of Socio-Economic and Cultural Paradigms*, pp. 251–71, Leuven: Leuven University Press.

Althaus-Reid, M. 1998b, 'Reconciliation in the Struggle: Theological Reflections from the Rebellious Women of Latin America', in Butler, B., ed., *Open Hands: Reconciliation, Justice and Peace Work Around the World*, pp. 397–411, Bury St Edmunds: Kevin Mayhew.

Althaus-Reid, M., 1998c, 'Towards an Indecent Theology for Times of Development Impasse: Economic Erections, Global Erections', *Ministerial Formation*, 81, pp. 4–11.

Althaus-Reid, M., 2000a, 'Grace and the Other: A Postcolonial Reflection on Ideology and Doctrinal Systems", in Wolde, E. J. V., ed., *The Bright Side of Life*, pp. 63–9, London: SCM Press.

Althaus-Reid, M., 2000b, 'Indecent Exposures: Excessive Sex and the Crisis of Theological Representation', in Isherwood, L., ed., *The Good News of the Body: Sexual Theology and Feminism*, pp. 205–22, New York: New York University Press.

Althaus-Reid, M., 2000c, *Indecent Theology: Theological Perversions in Sex, Gender and Politics*, New York: Routledge.

Althaus-Reid, M., 2000d, 'Re-writing God by Cancelling the Sex Debt in Theology: A Response to Clare Herbert's "Who is God for You?"', *Feminist Theology*, 8:23, pp. 31–5.

Althaus-Reid, M., 2001a, 'The Divine Exodus of God: Involuntary Marginalized, Taking an Option for the Margins, or Truly Marginal?', in Jeanrond, W. G. and C. Theobald, eds, *God, Experience and Mystery*, pp. 27–33, London: SCM Press.

Althaus-Reid, M., 2001b, 'Outing Theology: Thinking Christianity Out of the Church Closet', *Feminist Theology*, 9:27, pp. 57–67.

Althaus-Reid, M., 2003a, 'Bible of the Fracasados: Readings from the Excluded', in Oduyoye, M. A. and H. M. Vroom, eds, *One Gospel – Many Cultures: Case Studies and Reflections on Cross-Cultural Theology*, pp. 199–224, Amsterdam: World Alliance of Reformed Churches.

Althaus-Reid, M., 2003b, 'On Non-Docility and Indecent Theologians: A Response to the Panel for Indecent Theology', *Feminist Theology*, 11:2, pp. 182–9.

Althaus-Reid, M., 2003c, *The Queer God*, New York: Routledge.

Althaus-Reid, M., 2003d, 'Veníamos de Otras Tierras: A Reflection on Diasporas, Liberation Theology and Scotland', in Storrar, W. and P. Donald, eds, *God in Society: Doing Social Theology in Scotland Today*, pp. 126–35, Edinburgh: St Andrews Press.

Althaus-Reid, M., 2004a, 'El Tocado (Le Toucher): Sexual Irregularities in the Translation of God (The Word) in Jesus', in Sherwood, Y. and K. Hart, eds, *Derrida and Religion: Other Testaments*, pp. 393–405, New York: Routledge.

Althaus-Reid, M., 2004b, *From Feminist Theology to Indecent Theology*, London: SCM Press.

Althaus-Reid, M., 2004c, 'In the Centre there are No Fragments: Teologias Desencajados (Reflections on Unfitting Theologies)', in Storrar, W. F. and A. R. Morton, eds, *Public Theology for the 21st Century: Essays in Honour of Duncan B. Forrester*, pp. 365–83, London: T&T Clark.

Althaus-Reid, M., 2004d, '"Pussy, Queen of Pirates": Acker, Isherwood and the Debate on the Body in Feminist Theology', *Feminist Theology*, 12:2, pp. 157–67.

Althaus-Reid, M., 2004e, 'Queer I Stand: Lifting the Skirts of God', in Althaus-Reid, M. and L. Isherwood, eds, *The Sexual Theologian: Essays on Sex, God and Politics*, pp. 99–109, London: T&T Clark International.

Althaus-Reid, M., 2005a, 'Becoming Queens: Bending Gender and Poverty on the Websites of the Excluded', in Borgman, E., S. V. Erp and H. Haker, eds, *Cyberspace-Cyberethics-Cybertheology*, pp. 99–108, London: SCM Press.

Althaus-Reid, M., 2005b, 'From Liberation Theology to Indecent Theology', in Petrella, I., ed., *Latin American Liberation Theology: The Next Generation*, pp. 20–38, New York: Orbis Books.

Althaus-Reid, M., 2005c, 'From the Goddess to Queer Theology: The State We Are in Now', *Feminist Theology*, 13:2, pp. 265–72.

Althaus-Reid, M., 2006a, 'Education for Liberation', *Studies in World Christianity*, 12:1, pp. 1–4.

Althaus-Reid, M., 2006b, 'Graffiti on the Walls of the Cathedral of Buenos Aires: Doing Theology, Love and Politics at the Margins', in Hoelzl, M. and G. Ward, eds, *Religion and Political Thought*, London: Continuum.

Althaus-Reid, M., 2006c, 'On Dying Hard: Lessons from Popular Crucifixions and Undisciplined Resurrections in Latin America', in Queiruga, A. T., L. C. Susin and J. Sobrino, eds, *The Resurrection of the Dead*, pp. 35–43, London: SCM Press.

Althaus-Reid, M., 2006d, '"A Saint and a Church for Twenty Dollars": Sending Radical Orthodoxy to Ayacucho', in Ruether, R. R., M. Grau and M. Althaus-Reid, eds, *Interpreting the Postmodern: Responses to 'Radical Orthodoxy'*, pp. 107–18, New York: T&T Clark.

Althaus-Reid, M., 2007a, 'Class, Sex and the Theologian: Reflections on the Liberationist Movement in Latin America', in Althaus-Reid, M., I. Petrella and L. C. Susin, eds, *Another Possible World*, pp. 23–38, London: SCM Press.

Althaus-Reid, M., 2007b, 'Demythologising Liberation Theology: Reflections on Power, Poverty and Sexuality', in Rowland, C., ed., *The Cambridge Companion to Liberation Theology*, pp. 123–36, Cambridge: Cambridge University Press.

Althaus-Reid, M., 2007c, 'Feetishism: The Scent of a Latin American Body Theology', in Burrus, V. and C. Keller, eds, *Towards a Theology of Eros: Transfiguring Passion at the Limits of Discipline*, pp. 134–52, Fordham: Fordham University Press.

Althaus-Reid, M., 2007d, 'Queering the Cross: The Politics of Redemption and the External Debt', *Feminist Theology*, 15:3, pp. 289–301.

Althaus-Reid, M., 2007e, 'Searching for a Queer Sophia-Wisdom: The Post-Colonial Rahab', in Isherwood, L., ed., *Patriarchs, Prophets and Other Villains*, pp. 128–40, London: Equinox Publishing.

Althaus-Reid, M., 2008a, 'The Bi/girl Writings: From Feminist Theology to Queer Theologies', in Isherwood, L. and K. McPhillips, eds, *Post-Christian Feminism: A Critical Approach*, pp. 105–16, Aldershot: Ashgate Publishing.

Althaus-Reid, M., 2008b, 'Mutilations and Restorations: Cosmetic Surgery in Christianity', in Althaus-Reid, M. and L. Isherwood, eds, *Controversies in Body Theology*, pp. 70–9, London: SCM Press.

Althaus-Reid, M., 2008c, 'On Queer Theory and Liberation Theology: The Irruption of the Sexual Subject in Theology', in Althaus-Reid, M., ed., *Homosexualities*, pp. 83–96, London: SCM Press.

Althaus-Reid, M., 2009a, 'Introduction', in Althaus-Reid, M., ed., *Liberation Theology and Sexuality*, pp. 1–4, London: SCM Press.

Althaus-Reid, M., 2009b, '"Let Them Talk ...!" Doing Liberation Theology from Latin American Closets', in Althaus-Reid, M., ed., *Liberation Theology and Sexuality*, pp. 5–18, London: SCM Press.

Althaus-Reid, M., 2011, 'Doing a Theology from Disappeared Bodies: Theology, Sexuality, and the Excluded Bodies of the Discourses of Latin America', in Briggs, S. and M. M. Fulkerson, eds, *The Oxford Handbook of Feminist Theology*, pp. 441–55, Oxford: Oxford University Press.

Althaus-Reid, M. and L. Isherwood, 2008, 'Slicing Women's Bodies: Christianity and the Cut, Mutilated and Cosmetically Altered Believers', in Althaus-Reid, M. and L. Isherwood, eds, *Controversies in Body Theology*, pp. 1–6, London: SCM Press.

Isherwood, L. and M. Althaus-Reid, 2004, 'Introduction: Queering Theology – Thinking Theology and Queer Theory', in Althaus-Reid, M. and L. Isherwood, eds, *The Sexual Theologian: Essays on Sex, God, and Politics*, pp. 1–15, London: T&T Clark International.

Musskopf, A., 2010, 'Cruising (with) Marcella', in Isherwood, L. and M. D. Jordan, eds, *Dancing Theology in Fetish Boots: Essays in Honour of Marcella Althaus-Reid*, pp. 228–39, London: SCM Press.

Shore-Goss, R., 2010, 'Dis/Grace-full Incarnation and the Dis/Gracefull Church: Marcella Althaus-Reid's vision of Radical Inclusivity', in Isherwood, L. and M. D. Jordan, eds, *Dancing Theology in Fetish Boots: Essays in Honour of Marcella Althaus-Reid*, pp. 1–16, London: SCM Press.

Index of Names and Subjects

9 780334 061625